P9-DTY-592

Travels with My Royal

The Basque Series

Books by Robert Laxalt

The Violent Land: Tales the Old Timers Tell

Sweet Promised Land

A Man in the Wheatfield

Nevada

In a Hundred Graves: A Basque Portrait

A Cup of Tea in Pamplona

Nevada: A Bicentennial History

The Basque Hotel

A Time We Knew: Images of Yesterday in the Basque Homeland

The Governor's Mansion

Child of the Holy Ghost

A Lean Year and Other Stories

Dust Devils

A Private War: An American Code Officer in the Belgian Congo

The Land of My Fathers: A Son's Return to the Basque Country

Time of the Rabies

Travels with My Royal: A Memoir of the Writing Life

TRAVELS WITH MY ROYAL
A Memoir of the Writing Life

ROBERT LAXALT

With a foreword by Cheryll Glotfelty

University of Nevada Press ▲▲ Reno & Las Vegas

Winner of the Wilbur S. Shepperson Humanities Book Award for 2001

This book is the recipient of the Wilbur S. Shepperson Humanities Book Award, which is given annually in his memory by the Nevada Humanities Committee and the University of Nevada Press. One of Nevada's most distinguished historians Wilbur S. Shepperson was a founding board member and long-time supporter of both organizations.

THE BASQUE SERIES

Series Editor: William A. Douglass

University of Nevada Press, Reno, Nevada 89557 USA

Copyright © 2001 by Robert Laxalt

All rights reserved

Manufactured in the United States of America

Design by Carrie House

Library of Congress Cataloging-in-Publication Data

Laxalt, Robert, 1923–2001

Travels with my royal : a memoir of the writing life /

Robert Laxalt ; with a foreword by Cheryll Glotfelty.

p. cm. — (The Basque series)

ISBN 0-87417-485-6 (hardcover)

1. Laxalt, Robert, 1923–2001. 2. Authors, American—20th
century—Biography. 3. Basque Americans—Biography.
4. Authorship. I. Title. II. Series

PS3562.A9525   Z469   2001

813'.54—dc21   00-012721

The paper used in this book meets the requirements of
American National Standard for Information Sciences—
Permanence of Paper for Printed Library Materials,
ANSI Z39.48-1984. Binding materials were selected for
strength and durability.

FIRST PRINTING

10 09 08 07 06 05 04 03 02 01

5 4 3 2 1

For Joyce
Helpmate and love
Every step of the way

Contents

Foreword

If a U.S. state could be said to have a royal family, that honor in Nevada must surely go to the Laxalts. An imposing brick building named for the Laxalts fronts the main quadrangle at the University of Nevada, Reno. The Governor's Mansion in Carson City has been home to the Laxalts while Paul Laxalt was governor. He later served as a U.S. senator and close friend and advisor to President Reagan. The refurbished federal building that graces Main Street in Carson City has been named the Paul Laxalt State Building. The Nevada telephone book lists half a dozen Laxalts as attorneys and doctors. Robert Laxalt, author of this memoir, was founding direc-tor of the University of Nevada Press, cofounder of the university's internationally known Center for Basque Studies, coorganizer of the first Basque fes-tival in the American West, and the first living in-ductee to the Nevada Writers Hall of Fame.

Astonishingly, the ascendancy of the Laxalt name has occurred in a single generation. When Robert and his siblings were young children they traveled around from sheep camp to sheep camp, living for a time in a dirt-floored cabin in the present-day ghost town of Bodie, California. Finally, their mother had had enough of this hardscrabble, itinerant life, and she put down one hundred dollars— saved from her cooking on sheep ranches—on a little hotel in the state capital of Carson City, Nevada. In this small town of two thousand the Laxalt family received a less than royal welcome. In the first years the hotel barely eked out a livelihood, until they caught on to the local practice of serving alcohol. During Prohibition, the Laxalts were scorned for being "bootleggers," this on top of taunts they had already endured for being Basque and herding sheep. Perhaps out of this early discrimination, coupled with their mother's driving insistence on education, arose in the Laxalt children the stubborn determination to succeed. The Laxalt story takes its place in immigrant legend: from rags to well-being, low repute to honor, powerlessness to prominence, and from "foreigners" to full-fledged Americans.

In the memoir before you, however, *Royal* refers not to the Laxalt family's distinguished place in Nevada, but, rather, to their old, manual typewriter, a portable Royal that Mrs. Laxalt purchased for her children on which to write their school themes. This humble typewriter, which Robert Laxalt still uses, has been faithfully conveying type to paper, letter by letter, in a staccato rhythm that has been sustained for more than half a century. In Monique Urza's beautiful *The Deep Blue Memory*, a memoir of growing up in Robert Laxalt's family, she recalls the sound of her father's typing:

[I]t was there always, in the early morning hours as we woke, in the late night as we slept, in the background as we played. It had its own rhythm: a steady, continuous rap . . . then a slower rap . . . then a stalling, uneven rap . . . then silence . . . then an endless silence . . . then explosion into a flurry of sound . . . then quiet again.

The writerly alchemy taking place behind that office door is vividly recalled in *Travels with My Royal.* In one scene, Laxalt recalls his struggle to write a book about his father's visit to the Basque homeland after a lifetime of sheepherding in America. He cannot seem to find a way into this story:

> I was about to give up. I told myself, one more time. If it doesn't work, I will give up. I sat myself down in front of my old Royal portable, inserted that awful blank piece of paper, and sat back in my chair.
>
> After a few moments, my hands unconsciously, without thought or guidance on my part, traveled up to the keyboard and punched out, in lowercase, mind you, this line: "My father was a sheepherder and his home was the hills." I sat back and looked at that line for five minutes before its import came home to me. Then I said to myself, "That's it. You've got a book."
>
> And I did. It started from there. The story felt itself along word by word, line by line, paragraph by paragraph, chapter by chapter. . . . The story found itself.

One can almost hear that trusty old Royal as it tapped out *Sweet Promised Land,* the book that won instant national acclaim, triggered a Basque pride movement across the American West, and has remained in print for more than forty years—an enduring parable of immigrant experience.

Robert Laxalt, working steadily, working passionately, working often in the dark hours of predawn, has hammered out seventeen books and hundreds of articles on that Royal, earning a host of literary awards, including Spain's Tambor de Oro Award, several American Library Association honors, a Golden Spur Award by the Western Writers of America, two New York Public Library selections, and a Pulitzer Prize nomination. This achievement is all the more remarkable when one realizes that for most of his writing career, Laxalt held a full-time day job and was devoted to his family, including his parents, uncles, aunts, cousins, five siblings, and his wife and their three children.

Although Laxalt family members took time away from his writing they just as often formed its subject or helped him gain access to secret stories, as in the case of *A Cup of Tea in Pamplona*—his novel about

Basque smugglers between France and Spain. Since family members become characters in his work, and family experiences often provide the narrative line, one learns quite a lot about Robert Laxalt from reading his oeuvre. In *The Basque Hotel,* for example, we learn about Laxalt's childhood in Carson City, including such character-forming events as his nearly fatal bout with rheumatic fever, his family's move from the little hotel to a large house in the "high-toned" section of town, and his initiation into sheepherding with his father, high in the Sierra Nevada. In *Sweet Promised Land* we learn about Laxalt's immigrant father, Dominique; in *Child of the Holy Ghost* we learn about his mother's background; and in *The Governor's Mansion* the spotlight is on Laxalt's brother Paul. Laxalt's two Nevada histories occasionally break out of objectivity to convey his love for the "other" Nevada, with its vast panoramas, tonic aroma of sagebrush, and roughhewn characters. Laxalt's several Basque Country books— notably *In a Hundred Graves* and *The Land of My Fathers*— describe his experiences and impressions from his trips to his family's homeland. And the recent *A Private War* is drawn from journals Laxalt kept when he served as a code officer in the Belgian Congo during World War II. Together, Laxalt's works form a composite picture of the man, a man strongly tied to family, closely identified with both his Basque heritage and his American citizenship, and powerfully attached to Nevada.

What we do not get in the journey through his books is an insight into Laxalt the writer. But, after coming to love Laxalt's writing, it is precisely this story—of Laxalt's writing life—that we most want to hear. Laxalt's readers must wonder why he was drawn to writing, how he first broke into print, how he supported himself in order to write, where the ideas for his books came from, what considerations went into their composition, and what he thinks of them now. *Travels with My Royal* relieves this curiosity by revealing Laxalt, the man behind the typewriter.

The first half of the memoir focuses on Laxalt's youth, college years, employment as a newspaper reporter, later position as director of news and publications at the University of Nevada (UN), and a simultaneous two-decade assignment as a writer for *National Geographic* magazine. Delightful vignettes in this section include "marking" sheep with his father; venturing into a whorehouse; observing post–World War II fraternity life at UN; preparing for a collegiate debate against communism; meeting his wife, Joyce; receiving death threats when he broke a story about mob activities at Lake Tahoe; riding with gauchos in Argentina; and confronting frozen typewriter keys in Saint-Jean-de-Luz, France.

While part 1 chronicles Laxalt's formative years—a portrait of the artist as a young Nevadan—part 2 recounts the formation of his major works. Here Laxalt's many followers will witness the conception, gestation, birth, and even afterbirth of his literary offspring. These pages are a delicious treat. Bearing in mind that Laxalt is now seventy-seven and in delicate health, with waning energy for public appearances, the reader recognizes the privilege these chapters afford to share a private cup of tea, as it were, with this literary master as he regales one with the stories behind the stories. Rarely are writers so candid about their intentions and their craft. At times one almost feels as if Laxalt is slipping us a key to unlock the secrets of his work. As such, these discussions serve as ideal companions to the major works. They are likely to be of keen interest to beginning writers, as Laxalt illustrates with examples the process of writing—keeping a journal, identifying a story, determining point of view, creating characters, setting a scene, layering a work, finding an ending.

After reading *Travels with My Royal* one wants to hasten back to the bookshelves to reread Laxalt's entire body of work. One wants to say, "Thank you. For everything." And one wants powerfully for his Royal to keep on beating.

—CHERYLL GLOTFELTY

Associate Professor, University of Nevada, Reno

GROWING UP

Bootlegging Days

IN THOSE DAYS, a restroom was known as a water closet. It derived its name from a wooden tank of water attached to the wall with a chain dangling from it. When one pulled the chain, the tank would empty with a roar of water that flushed the toilet.

My first memory is of being perched on my mother's knee when we were hiding in a water closet.

My mother was saying her rosary and admonishing my three brothers and two sisters and me not to shuffle our feet or talk above a whisper because the *prohis* were about. It was Prohibition time, and there was a quart of whiskey concealed in the water closet. We could hear the *prohis* walking in impolite steps on the wooden floor of the long dining room. The memory frightens me in my dreams to this day.

Nothing came of the incident that I can recall. The *prohis,* or prohibition agents, left, and in a little while, my mother went back to her kitchen and we children went out in the backyard to play.

I suppose this made us bootleggers, but hardly in the league of Al Capone and Joe Kennedy, who operated in grand style with fleets of trucks loaded with Scotch whiskey instead of poor man's bourbon.

They had hundreds of cases of whiskey. We had one case of twelve bottles at a time for the boarders in our little four-bedroom hotel and the customers who came for dinner.

Being bootleggers put us in a lower social standing, though I never could make the distinction between our serving whiskey and those who bought it— including the occupants of the Governor's Mansion and the opulent homes of supreme court justices.

We paid the penalty for it when our schoolmates called us bootleggers in accusatory tones that were a mark of shame. These were the children of men who

had drunk away their money in the saloon. Whenever this happened, I would blanch as the color left
my face, and I bowed my head like a criminal. I was
spared insult, though, by the son of the minister,
who simply looked at me querulously, as if to say,
"How could you sell whiskey?" I don't know which
penalty was worse. Though I had to be loyal to my
parents, I never could understand in the early days
how they could inflict such shame upon me.

The answer came clear later on, when I learned
that my father was forced into bootlegging by the
livestock depression that preceded the big one. My
father had been rich in sheep and cattle and ranches
when the crash came. Like most of the farmers and
ranchers in the United States, he lost nearly everything. Even then, he could have survived the crash
were it not for a winter of paralyzing cold that froze
more that two thousand ewes and lambs to death in
the northern deserts. All that he had left from the
rich days was a big car.

Jobs being hard to come by in the Depression, he
wandered from ranch to ranch in Nevada and
northern California taking what work there was. We
were living in a brown board shack with a dirt floor

in the ghost town of Bodie near the California state line when my mother decided that she had had enough of hard times. She had saved one hundred dollars from cooking on ranches during my father's wandering days from ranch to ranch. She heard through the Basque grapevine that a little boarding-house hotel of four bedrooms, a dining room, and a saloon was for sale in Carson City, Nevada, and promptly put her one hundred dollars down on it. Thus our move from a ramshackle ghost town to the state capital in Carson City.

Things looked promising for a while by reason of her cooking. She had actually studied at the Cordon Bleu cooking school in Paris. People came to sample her cooking, but it was not enough. Unless one served whiskey and wine with dinner, people went elsewhere.

I remember one night when my father accosted the sheriff on the street and asked him why he was sending visitors to Carson City to another little hotel like ours for dinner. The sheriff said that the visitors wanted a drink before dinner and wine with dinner, so he had no choice but to send them to the other hotel.

That was the night when my father decided to go into bootlegging. Contacting suppliers among the immigrant Italians and the Basques was no problem. They had stills for making whiskey and vats to make wine.

Deliveries were made at night. I went with my father one night to an arranged location on the highway between Carson City and Reno, thirty miles away. It was a black, black night, and the only lights were at faraway ranches in Washoe Valley. A man named Nikolas hoisted a couple of cases of whiskey and some kegs of wine from his truck to my father's spacious Nash. My father paid him in cash, and we went back to Carson City.

IT'S SAID THAT children's characters are shaped in part by the company their parents keep. If that is so, our personalities had a treasure trove to draw from. Customers at the hotel were living lessons for us. There was Old Vic, a prospector who lived in a shack between Carson and the Sierra, where his mine was located. Old Vic was always on the verge of finding a fortune, but it eluded him. Nevertheless, he never gave up hope. He managed to glean enough dust and tiny nuggets to keep himself alive. The big lode was always just around the corner. He was never defeated. As long as he found enough gold to keep himself in food and booze, he was happy. He taught me that a man doesn't need riches to be content with life.

Mizoo was a tall, rawboned cowboy who broke and sold mustangs that he caught in the hills. He was a master at telling tall tales about his exploits, and at charging his drinks. My mother wanted to cut off his credit, but Mizoo's stories at the long dinner table managed to entertain customers. We learned that the gift of gab can make up for hard cash in this world.

Then there were the politicians who came in after work for a shot or two of whiskey. For the most part, they paid for their booze, but even if they didn't, my mother calculated that their political influence in Prohibition times was worth the price. They were name-droppers all, of governors and senators and congressmen, and we learned that it was not what you knew that counted, but whom you knew. It was a lasting lesson.

The repeal of Prohibition ended the bootlegging era of our lives. My mother bought a home in the best part of Carson City, and my father bought a band of sheep and a truck and went back to his true calling.

When he did this, he thrust upon us as children the appellation of *sheepherder,* which also was not very high on the social scale. Again, I paid for it with the names and jokes inflicted upon me by my schoolmates. Though the sheep business went a long way in feeding and housing our family, I was again not grateful. It seemed to me that my parents were dead bent on humiliating me in this life. Nevertheless, I had to live with it. This was the beginning of our family's sheepherding days.

Sheepherding Days

MY MOTHER NEVER had much to do with my father's going into the sheep business. Her interest lay in properties. She leased the French Hotel to a Basque couple who knew what was involved in running a little hotel, serving meals, and—now that Prohibition was repealed—operating a saloon.

Actually, the saloon was the fanciest part of an otherwise plain wooden hotel with a false front. It had a long mahogany bar with a shiny brass foot rail, with spaced spittoons, a back bar well stocked with dozens of kinds of liquor—half of it for show—a huge mirror with a mahogany frame, and on the customer's side a hand-painted mural that covered an entire wall. It depicted a mine with all its accompaniments—a massive hole in the hillside from which a little ore train emerged, a mill with smoking chimney stacks, and an array of humanity, such as miners with picks and shovels, mill workers, and even feathered Indians peering out from the forest that overlooked this scene of furious white man's activities.

The painted canvas bore a slash from a knife, a souvenir of a legendary knife fight in the hotel's early days.

It took a while for our neighbors to accept our being immigrants in an Anglo-Saxon part of town and our having been bootleggers before. But time and good behavior overcame that, and when we proved to be good students in school, altar boys, and good athletes as well, we were accepted as part of the community.

I saw little of my father after he went back into the sheep business, but he was a busy man with a lot of things to put together, buying grazing land for summer range in the Sierra and getting permits to graze on the public domain between the private parcels he had bought. We were of little use to him in the sheep business until we were in high school and old enough to help him in the busy times of the sheep year, such as marking and shearing.

Marking time, I suppose, could have been traumatic, but my father did not know what the word meant. One day he simply told my older brother and me that he needed our help, bundled us into his big stake truck, and took us to the rundown ranch that served as headquarters for his sheep business. We left our home and Carson City dressed in our most ragged clothes in preparation for what was to come. And we hunkered down in the cab of the big truck so that our friends who happened to be about would not see us.

Marking time is an occasion for Basque sheep owners to gather. Everyone is expected to help out, visiting with each other while they help herd sheep into the maze of corrals and wooden chutes used for separating lambs from mothers while the marking and docking went on. The ewes or mother sheep were crowded into the long wooden chute, at the end of which there was what was called a dodge gate that swung from right to left. When the sheep came down the chute, the lambs were shunted into one small corral and the mothers into a big corral.

At one end of the small corral, there was a huge tablelike plank thoroughly saturated with blood from previous markings. Behind the block was one of the visiting men chosen for his strong teeth. He was armed with a long pocketknife whose blade had been polished to a razor sharpness. At his feet, there were two containers, one to hold the lambs' tails and the other to contain testicles from the wether or male lambs. The wether lambs had to be castrated, not only to make their meat less strong in flavor but also to keep them from growing into rams.

My brother's and my job was to catch the lambs, double their legs, and plant their rear ends on the marking block while the operation was performed.

It was not altogether a simple process. The marking man had no problem lopping off the tails of the lambs for facility in breeding and also to keep count on how many lambs were marked. For my brother and me, cutting off the tails was the most hazardous part of the operation. When the tail was cut off, a thin stream of blood shot into the air. There was no predicting what direction the stream would spurt. I ducked my head from one side to the other, but inevitably, it seemed, I ducked the wrong way and the blood would spurt into my face. After an hour, I was as bloody as an axe murderer.

When the lamb's tail had been cut off, I held the male lambs in place for castration.

Since lamb testicles are so small, the marking man had to perform the vital part of the operation with his teeth. He sliced off the end of the lamb's scrotum, set the knife aside, and squeezed with thumb and forefinger. The testicles, which resembled tiny sausages, emerged, and the marking man seized them with his teeth and pulled them out, then dropped them into the second container at his feet.

Finally, I tipped the lamb forward, and the marking man performed the last part of the operation, notching a mark into the lamb's ear for identification. Our mark was an undercut on the left ear.

Naturally, the lambs were as weak as kittens when it was over. I handed mine gently to one of the helpers in the main corral, and he carried the lamb to the protection of the fence line, where it called for its mother. When she came, she lay down beside her lamb until it had enough strength to reach a teat for strength-giving milk. I marveled at the shortness of recovery time. In a few minutes, the lamb was suckling at its mother's udder. Strength came back almost immediately, and in a little while, the lamb was tottering about.

And so it went for the rest of the day. When the lambs had all been marked, one of the Basques washed the testicles thoroughly, then dropped them into a huge Dutch oven with olive oil. Peppers and garlic were added, then a dozen eggs. I had never imagined eating lamb fries, as they are called, but I ate them now with bread and wine and appetite.

I was soaked with drying blood from hair to shoes, but my father paid it no more attention than if I had had on my Sunday suit.

This was the life of the sheepherder, and I had had my first taste of it. On the way home in the truck, I began to understand the life my father led and wondered if I would be expected to do the same. Perhaps it was because I was young, and the young accept the turns of life so easily, but oddly enough the prospect did not repel me.

A Polite Town

AS FAR AS WESTERN towns went, Carson City was a polite town. From the time I was a young boy, I said hello to everyone I met on Main Street and they said hello to me. Nobody said I had to. It was just the accepted thing to do, from the governor on down to the town drunk who swamped out the whorehouses just off Main Street.

Carson City wasn't a poor town, but it wasn't a rich town either. Reno was where the people who had gotten rich off the silver and gold mines went to bank their money and build mansions overlooking the Truckee River.

The fact that Carson was a small town obviously had something to do with it. I could walk from one city limit to the other in half an hour. Main Street meant a grocery store, a butcher shop, a shoe store, a clothing store for men and one for women, a couple of cafés, the pool hall, a hardware store, and five saloons. Interspersed between them were the ponderous stone buildings that housed the courthouse, the U.S. Post Office, the State Library, a one-time U.S. Mint, the depot where the Virginia and Truckee short-line railway stopped, and of course, in the middle of town, the State Capitol of Nevada with its spiraling dome and winding balconies in a setting of sprawling green lawns and dark elms.

To find someone's house, it really wasn't necessary to know all the street signs, because houses were identified by their occupants, not their location. The west side was the high-toned part of town, spreading down from the Governor's Mansion. Its gracious lawns and flower gardens lay under a canopy of cottonwood trees, and the western edge of town was defined by a long line of sentinel poplars to blunt the force of the winds that swept down from the Sierra.

The east side of Carson held smaller homes, and beyond them were the Indian shacks, Chinatown until it was burned down by design of the volunteer fire department, the Orphans Home, and the grim stone outlines of the Nevada State Prison.

On Main Street, people who worked in government wore suits, neckties, and hats. Their wives wore proper dresses and summer frocks and hats. The so-called working class wore blue overalls; the ranchers wore high boots and big hats; Indian men wore cast-off clothes, and their women who sat against the buildings on Main Street wrapped themselves in blankets to help the sun warm their old bones.

The merchants on Main Street were singular characters. My favorite was old Bert Lindsay, who owned the bakery and grocery store. He was a gangling, gray-haired man who wore wire-rimmed glasses perched on his nose so that he could look down through them when he was doing his accounting and over them when he was talking to people. He wore a wrinkled shirt with arm garters and a bow tie, but no coat. He perched on a high stool beside his high desk so that he could keep an eye on his help and the people who came in to buy doughnuts and bear claws and such or a can of something they couldn't find elsewhere.

In the one summer I worked there doing odd jobs, he would call on me to come to him for an admonition: "If you're going to smoke when you're a man, don't smoke cigarettes. They're for pimps. Smoke cigars. They are for men." He would end his ritual by blowing cigar smoke in my face and then go back to his accounting. Later, when I read Dickens, I likened old man Lindsay to one of the many accountants in high chairs that worked in old London Town.

Buck Muller was my second favorite merchant on Main Street. He ran a clothing store that catered to men only. He had a poker face and always wore a derby hat when he went outdoors. What intrigued and puzzled me about him was that everyone said he was the best liar in Nevada. This created a contradiction in my mind that lasted through my childhood on Main Street. I thought people meant he was a bad man whose word was not to be trusted. It wasn't until much later that I learned there was a society of liars in every town, and that Buck Muller had earned his distinction as a champion liar through the tall tales he told in the tradition of Mark Twain. Twain had lived in Carson City for a spell during his Nevada Territorial days when his brother was secretary to the governor of the territory, and he was known for the tall tales he wrote for Virginia City's *Territorial Enterprise.*

The man I worked with was named Blarney. He was in his twenties and a prototype of Carson City "boys" who went from high school with no ambitions but to get a job, usually in menial labor, and make enough money to get drunk on Saturday night and go to the whorehouses. Others, more ambitious, went on to work in one of the state departments.

Blarney's job in the store where we worked was to wash the windows after work and to haul up canned goods from the basement and stock the shelves. When I wasn't called upon to man the sales counter, my job was to help Blarney with his chores.

Because I wanted a future higher than holding down a menial job and getting drunk on Saturday night and going to the whorehouses, Blarney didn't take a liking to me. I was the butt of his jokes and jibes.

I was a little afraid of him because he did crazy things. Periodically, he would take a bite out of a beer glass or burn a prostitute's initials into his arm with a glowing cigarette. Once, he was bitten by a black widow spider in the store basement. He refused to go to a doctor and kept on working with a swollen leg.

When World War II came, he was drafted and went into action as an infantryman. When he returned, he was a changed man—freshly shaven, trimly uniformed, and standing upright. Across his chest was a row of medals for heroism in combat. From his standing as town bum, he was suddenly a hero, leaving me to wonder what was the stuff of heroes.

Altar Boys

FROM THE TIME we graduated into high school, the sons of Catholic parents were expected to be altar boys at St. Theresa's Catholic Church.

We were subject to the authority of a succession of Irish priests with names like Murphy, Ryan, and O'Grady. There were so many that I began to believe all priests everywhere were born in Ireland and spoke with a brogue.

On Sundays, we took turns serving Mass, at either eight o'clock or ten o'clock. We gathered in the sacristy and donned red cassocks and white surplices. The masses were said in Latin and so were our memorized responses, which, coupled with the burning of incense and pouring water and wine for the priests, cast a mystical aura over the services. *Dominus vobiscum* and *et cum spiritu tuo* were a part of our vocabulary.

The only compensation for altar boys were *indulgences,* which I took to be credits toward heaven. We served without pay, except for weddings and funerals, where it was expected that we be paid by either the best man or the family of the bereaved. When it came to funerals, we earned every penny of our gratuity. Tears and heartbreak were grim ordeals for teenage boys.

Otherwise, being an altar boy was a good experience. Sunday masses were something of an ordeal, but morning masses, little attended, brought a feeling of peace that lasted for the day. It eased us through the travails that beset us during school days.

Town Characters

EVERY SMALL TOWN has its characters, and
Carson City was no exception in the years when we
were ensconced in my mother's little French Hotel.

They were less in evidence when we moved to our
family home in the respectable west side of Carson
City.

At the French Hotel, little Tip the Irishman
started our days bright and early. As soon as the
saloon opened, he was there in his shallow derby
hat and bow tie. He perched himself at the end of
the long bar and held up his hand, thumb and

forefinger touching, in a signal for "a short one."
No words were necessary.

Once served, Tip would nurse his shot glass of
whiskey with solemnity, staring into its amber
depths all the while he drank.

When he was finished, he would sigh, place a coin
on the bar, and say to all, "The top o' the mornin'
to ye."

Once I asked him why he drank in the morning
instead of at the end of the day like most of the men
did. Tip said the shot of whiskey was his "eye opener"
and added, "It gets the blood movin'." Then, tipping
his hat, he was gone.

George Washington Lopez was another regular.
He was a man with the most doleful expression I
have ever seen. And he was flat-footed, so that when
he came into the saloon, it was to the accompani-
ment of flapping feet.

George Washington Lopez, or "Wash" as he was
universally known, was the swamper at Nigger
Ruby's whorehouse a block away from the State
Capitol. As such, he knew the latest news about "a
new girl" at the whorehouse, and which of the

town's dignitaries partook of Ruby's wares the night before.

There were others, like Mickey McCluskey, the prospector who was Carson City's whiskey-drinking Santa Claus. Mickey McCluskey was a cheerful soul who would respond to a greeting with "I'm feelin' fine and doozy." His visits to the saloon were timed to runs of good luck in his pick-and-shovel gold-mining pit in the nearby Sierra.

Then there were others like Mizoo, the horse trader who had to be watched when he was near the cash register, and Pansy Gifford, the handyman who always wore a pansy in his lapel.

My favorite character was Buckshot Dooney, the town drunk. Buckshot was singular in his attire. He wore striped, paint-spattered overalls and a battered derby hat. His face was flushed, and he always sported a stubble of black beard.

Buckshot was Carson City's exclusive confidence man. Any scheme that would garner him drinking money was his to ply. The unsuspecting folk of Carson City were fair game.

Buckshot's most lucrative scheme was when a floor covering called linoleum came on the market.

With his gaily colored roll of linoleum tucked under his arm, Buckshot went door-to-door down the back streets of Carson City. He fared well, not only because of his gift of Irish gab, but also because linoleum was a legitimate commodity. It was the answer to worn wooden floors. Buckshot's wallet swelled.

Impatient customers were to wait in vain. When the delivery date passed, they began looking for Buckshot, to no avail. Buckshot had disappeared.

No one ever knew where Buckshot vanished to in his timely absences. Word had it that he spent his hideaway time in one of the opium dens in Chinatown. He came back to town when tempers had cooled and the good people of Carson City accepted the fact that they had been taken in again.

Buckshot's reputation reached its zenith when he served a brief apprenticeship as an undertaker. It came about this way:

Buckshot was the ne'er-do-well son of a respectable Carson family, who from time to time took pity on him. His brother was a mortician, the only one in Carson. He offered Buckshot a job, laying down strict rules of appearance and conduct. One day,

Buckshot made his way downtown clean-shaven and dressed in a suit. The transformation was something to behold.

It was during Buckshot's tenure as an undertaker that a man from Chinatown died. In those days, the Chinese took it upon themselves to ship the body back to China to rest with its ancestors. The Chinaman (as he was called then) was delivered to Buckshot's brother's mortuary and entrusted to Buckshot's tender care, his brother being absent on a trip to San Francisco.

The body was embalmed, put in a proper casket, and shipped off to China. When the body arrived in China, all hell broke loose. Cables of protest and indignation were sent to the U.S. government, Nevada state government, and Carson City officialdom.

The outrage was justified.

The Chinese who died had been a tall man, unusual for his race. When his body was turned over to the mortuary, Buckshot found himself in a quandary. He had already made a coffin suited in size to the average Oriental. The Chinaman simply would not fit.

But fit he did after Buckshot got through with him. Buckshot had neatly cut off his legs at the knees, laid them gently beside the body, and shipped the coffin off.

Peace was finally restored, but Buckshot had no part in the peacemaking. He had disappeared again.

When he next graced the streets of Carson City, Buckshot was his old self—black-bearded, wearing paint-spattered overalls and a battered derby hat, and unemployed.

Growing Up

AT FIRST, OUR NEIGHBORS didn't quite know what to make of us. I suppose that was to be expected. This was the old heart of Carson City, and the families who lived there had been settled for a long time.

Also, they were Anglo-Saxons and we, or at least our parents, were Basque immigrants. The men wore neckties to work, and our father dressed in Levi's. In church, my mother said her prayers in French, to my embarrassment. I came to dread the ending of the Lord's Prayer. Everyone else said "Amen," but she said "Ainsi soit-il."

The men of our neighborhood held political offices and state government jobs for the most part, Carson City being the state capital, or else they owned stores on Main Street. My parents, as everyone knew, had owned and run a little hotel with a false front, and they had sold liquor on the side.

To have as neighbors immigrants who once ran a saloon did not sit well with the respectable occupants of the fine houses in our neighborhood. They never said so openly, but the pause in their hellos spelled out what they were thinking.

In time, this sort of mild discrimination wore away. They had to get used to us. But the main impetus behind our acceptance was that my brothers and sisters and I were on the school honor rolls faithfully printed in the *Carson City Daily Appeal.* Also, we brothers were good athletes on varsity high school teams, which counted for a lot in the small towns of Nevada. It was the passport to acceptance, both in school and downtown.

Pool Hall Days

FROM THE DAY we graduated into high school, Berger's Pool Hall was our second home, Carson City having no recreation hall for boys.

The pool hall, or pool shack as we boys familiarly called it, was located on Main Street in the center of town. It had a nondescript front with big windows and double doors. There was no need for a sign, since everybody in town knew where it was.

Inside, there was a long, scarred bar where the men drank beer after their jobs in the offices of government departments such as highways, public service, and printing. The buildings all looked the same, built of stone from the prison quarry, with wide steps leading up to tall doors and wide stairways. The State Capitol dominated all, being the tallest building in town. It was surrounded by green sweeps of lawn, flower gardens, and elm trees that had been planted when Nevada was admitted to the Union in 1864.

Schoolboys played mumblety-peg on the lawns, which were scarce in Carson City, and old-timers sat on the green benches outside the scrollworked wrought-iron fence.

The unquestioned lord and master of the pool hall was a jovial and kindly man named "Dutch" Glansman. He wore a wide apron for tending bar and dispensing beer from the taps that spewed forth Tahoe beer, which was the product of the huge brewery across from the schoolhouse, also made of prison stone. It was the only school in town, instructing both grammar and high school students. Teachers were mostly stern women with pompadour hairdos. The school was nestled among a cluster of churches—Catholic, Presbyterian, and Episcopalian.

The mix of patrons of the pool hall included workingmen and high school boys. The men came to play pool and drink beer in moderate portions from sturdy glasses and steins. How much they drank depended upon their pocket money and Dutch's dictates. He brooked no nonsense. Too much drink and foul language were not permitted, and nobody under the age of twenty-one drank beer. If we boys had any money, which was seldom, we drank root beer and Coca-Cola.

After work, the two massive pool tables were taken over by the young bucks of the town. But between the after-school hours of three and five, the high school boys dominated the play for free, rotation and snooker mostly. No betting was allowed for the young—another of Dutch's dictates.

Parents of the boys who inhabited the pool hall knew they had no need to worry. Dutch came from an old Carson City family that held proper conduct supreme. When eight o'clock came, Dutch sent all the boys home. If they dallied along the way, Dutch heard about it and banned the culprits for as long as a week—a frightful penalty.

At the far end of the pool hall, there was a huge potbellied stove around which the old-timers sat and visited with each other and played solo on a card table covered with worn oilcloth. Most of the old-timers were widowers or bachelors with nowhere else to go. They lived in shacks and boardinghouses in the poor parts of town. In winter, they made a welcome sight and for me a source of stories about the old days in Carson. I suspect that half of the stories were exaggerations, but they made good listening.

The potbellied stove did not hurt for fuel. It burned leftover copies of the *Reno Evening Gazette* and the *San Francisco Chronicle,* which were hand-rolled and distributed by Berger's pool hall, coming by stage from Reno. The newspapers were rolled on the pool hall's long bar by the old-timers and the young men after work, then carried outside to an old open sedan that roared down the back streets, from which they would be thrown onto front lawns and yards. They sometimes hit people who were not alert enough when they walked out of their front doors. And sometimes they would flatten a prize rose in a garden. But all in all, they managed to wreak only minor havoc. The delivery process took about an hour, and everyone who helped got a free glass of beer from Dutch's tap. Officeholders helped out, too, and sometimes even the governor.

The pool hall had as much to do with our bringing up as school and church. I can think of worse places to grow up, such as the whorehouses, but that would not be fair.

Carson City had three whorehouses, all legal under Nevada law, grouped together on a back street only two blocks from the Capitol. They were more like social centers than dens of iniquity, places for state workers to gather for a drink before going home.

The houses were known familiarly as Five, Six, and Seven. I assume that One, Two, Three, and Four existed in Carson's more prosperous days, but I never knew for sure.

Bachelors, statehouse visitors, and traveling salesmen made up most of the business, but a few of the older, more daring, and prosperous high school students also patronized them on Saturday nights.

Unable to bear any more taunts about being chicken, I succumbed and went to a whorehouse with two of my schoolmates on a Saturday night that is still stamped indelibly on my memory. The first thing I remember about my visit was the heady fragrance of perfume that enveloped me as I walked through the front door. It sent me into a dreamlike state of mind that, coupled with fear, made me weak in the knees. I did not, could not resist the pushes from my friends, who were enjoying this initiation to the hilt.

Once inside, I was surrounded by grown-up men, some in suits and others in work clothes, and flimsily clad girls wandering through the crowd. There was an empty chair near the front door, and I seized it desperately. I clasped the arms of the chair and stared at the floor, hoping that I was invisible.

My so-called friends, who were seniors in high school, made sure that I would not remain invisible. A girl in a gauzy dress walked up to my chair, murmured hello in a dulcet voice, and sat down on my lap. I was terrified and speechless, looking up only once into a powdered face with red lipstick, mascaraed eyes, and blond curls.

One of my friends leaned down to my ear and said, "We'll pay the two-and-a-half bucks if you'll turn a trick with Daisy." I could not answer in my paralysis. Not wanting to hurt Daisy's feelings, I shook my head and said nothing. The next thing I knew, she had taken me by the hand and raised me to my feet, intending to take me to her crib.

If I were older, I would have succumbed, but I was too young and powerless. I disengaged my hand from Daisy's and made a dash for the door. Once outside, I ran all the way home.

My friends never let me forget my failure to prove myself a man. But my time would come.

Home

O U R   H O U S E   W A S   a haven. When things had gone
wrong during the day, it was there I went to find
refuge and solace.

When I had passed through the gate that divided
the two stands of tall hedge, gone up the walkway to
the screened porch with its hanging swing and oaken
rocking chairs, I found the first measure of reassurance.

To find the full measure, I had to pass through
the ornate, glass-paned front door and enter the
sanctuary of high-ceilinged rooms that lay beyond.

The foyer with its long mission-style bookcase

(which rests in my study now) spoke of a family that read, and in that, more reassurance. The living room with its lofty ceiling and bay window came next on my route, and after that, the dining room with its long mission table where we ate our meals and did our homework.

The kitchen that was my destination was the heart of the house, filled with tantalizing kitchen smells. My mother's presence radiated from it. Standing by her big stove with her warm smile and graying hair caught up in back in a chignon, she would greet me.

I would respond, "Hi, Mom." I'd give the world to be able to speak those words today.

When we were growing up, my mother would bake bread on Saturdays, and the yeasty scent of it would waft over the neighborhood, a sure lure for our playmates to come to have a piece of bread still warm from the oven.

Dinners were the high point of the day. My three brothers and two sisters would gather at the table for my mother's French soups, beef and lamb stews, and french-fried potatoes, or chops carved from the lamb that hung in the coolness of the attic stairwell.

My older brother, Paul, crew-cut and wearing his

C letter sweater for sports, usually sat at the head of the table. Then came my hazel-eyed sister Suzanne, already wearing the reserve that would guide her into becoming a nun. Then my sister Marie, with her infectious smile and luxuriant auburn hair. My brother John, tall and giving promise of becoming a star basketball player, came next. And finally my brother Peter, the scholar of the family.

It was here that we shared with each other what had happened during the school day, offered advice and received it, and learned what was new in the world of sports.

Out of old-country custom, my mother never joined us at the table, feeling it her duty to feed her family first.

It was a rare treat when my father—sheepcamp obligations allowing him a night of surcease—would have dinner with us. Lean and bronzed and silvering, wearing Levi's and a clean khaki shirt, he regaled us with stories of what was going on in the hills.

Sometimes, he would have with him a young sheepherder newly arrived from the Basque Country, attired in new Levi's and workshirt. The herders were invariably bashful and unable to speak English, so my father spoke to them in Basque.

After dinner, my mother would permit herself to sit at the table with us and speak in Basque with a young herder, who was invariably from her part of the Basque Country.

In those interludes, our ears were filled with the rich Basque tongue, only a little of which we could understand. But the flavor was enough.

Memories like this went to make up the healing when I was bone hurt, leaving me clean and un-afraid of the world.

My Two Uncle Petes

I HAD TWO Uncle Petes who shuttled in and out of my young years.

One uncle's real name was Jean Pierre, Petya in Basque. He had emigrated from France at about the turn of the century. He came as a sheepherder and worked for sheep instead of wages, which was the custom among Basques in those early range days.

In time, he built a herd of his own. He broke off from the sheepman who had paid his passage and grazed the public domain or open range. When my father came to America, he followed the same order of things. In time, they combined herds and became partners. In his free time, my uncle was taken with the lure of the cowboy myth and became a roper at the rodeos they encountered. Eventually, he tired of the sheep business and sold his part of the herd to my father, who had decided to stay in the business.

This Uncle Pete was a bachelor and a gentle man. He believed, like my father, that horses should be broken with gentleness. I am not sure why he never married. Perhaps it was because he moved back and forth between sheep and cattle jobs and never had a ranch of his own. He said that being a bachelor was like the life of a "lonely coyote." That was probably the reason he lived with us from time to time—so that he could be with family and children.

Every Sunday, he would exchange boots and Levi's for his suit, complete with necktie. After Mass, he would go out in front of the house and sit in my father's pickup to watch the people go by. In the family, he was known as the gentle Uncle Pete.

NOT SO WITH my other Uncle Pete, who was a hard man. He had served in the Zouaves, the mounted unit of the French Foreign Legion in Af–

rica, which probably contributed to his regimented, unforgiving nature.

He came to America and became a cattleman near Susanville, just across the Nevada state line. He was known as a superb horseman, able to stand on the back of a horse at full gallop, a trick he had learned in the Zouaves.

My father did not approve of the way his brother trained horses, bucking them out until they were broken. "I don't want to speak against my brother," my father would say, "but I will tell you this. If a hoss wasn't mean when he got him, he was mean when he got rid of him."

My Uncle Pete from Madeleine was noted for other attributes, too—fighting with his neighbors and being hard on his two sons, Gabriel and Robert.

My cousin Gabriel, the eldest son, recounted to me the ordeal he had to endure whenever his father announced that they were going to "ride range" next day to check on the stock.

Uncle Pete could not tolerate his sons getting bucked off a horse. To avoid his father's wrath,

Gabriel would get out of bed in the middle of the night, sneak down to the horse corral, and pick out the horse he would be riding the next day. Since Uncle Pete's horses were all "buckers," Gabriel would pick out one that would hurt him the least, saddle him, and let go. Expectedly, the horse would throw Gabriel off, not once but two or three times. When the horse was bucked out, Gabriel could be reasonably assured of a tolerable ride the next day. His father never spoke of the bruises on Gabriel's face.

Uncle Pete from Madeleine had a running feud with a neighbor cattleman. The neighbor's calf had gotten mixed up with my uncle's herd. Branding time was upon them, and Uncle Pete told his neighbor to cull out his calf so that there wouldn't be any mistakes the next day. The neighbor did not, probably on purpose. But he was a witness to all the confusion and bustle of branding time, and he was there when my uncle accidentally branded his calf. The neighbor accosted my uncle and accused him of stealing his calf. My Uncle Pete settled the dispute by pulling his carbine out of its scabbard and shooting the calf dead. "He's nobody's calf now," he announced.

The neighbor brought charges, but my Uncle Pete refused to apologize or pay for the calf. The judge fined him and sentenced him to two months in jail.

The penalty did not faze my Uncle Pete from Madeleine one bit. He walked out of jail as arrogantly as he had gone in.

His family refused to forgive him. Without telling anyone, Uncle Pete went to the bank, drew out his money, and deposited it under a false name in some bank in California. After he died, a search for the money proved fruitless. My Uncle Pete had wreaked his revenge for not being forgiven.

Uncle Pete from Madeleine was a hard man, indeed.

Hero Worship

THE GYMNASIUM WAS a bedlam, the applause deafening. The score was tied. There were only two minutes remaining in the game.

Caesar and Geno—their names were always linked—were bringing the ball down the court. Geno, who was the smaller of the two, was a master dribbler. Twisting and turning, he crossed the center line into enemy Reno territory.

When he calculated that he had penetrated the Reno defense far enough, he passed the ball to Caesar, who was waiting on the outskirts of the Reno defense. Caesar grasped the basketball with two hands and raised it to his chest.

The heart-stopping moment was at hand, and the Carson fans suddenly fell quiet. Caesar crouched a little and sent the ball toward the Reno basket in a high arc. The two-handed shot was his specialty, and the ball dropped through the rim and swished into the netting. The whistle shrilled and the game was over. Carson had beaten mighty Reno High School eighteen to sixteen.

The Carson fans poured onto the court in a frenzy of emotion. Caesar and Geno were lifted onto the shoulders of the crowd and paraded around the gymnasium floor.

Hero worship was an integral part of my high school days. Who could experience such a dramatic victory without becoming infected?

It follows that Caesar and Geno were Carson City's heroes, and I was one of their worshipers. The fact that they were Orphan Home kids did not demean them a bit.

They led Carson to state championships three years in succession. I was not alone in worshiping the ground they walked on. The businessmen of Carson bought them their blue letter sweaters adorned with four stripes, one for each varsity year, and three stars, one for each of the state championships they had led Carson to.

No wonder that my secret dreams were to score a winning basket or a winning touchdown that would give me the right to wear a letter sweater. When finally, in my senior year, I played the required quarters and could wear a letter sweater, I felt exalted to the heavens.

These days, hero worship is on the wane. Perhaps it is because there are too many stars on television, or too many stars who have through indiscretion become fallen idols. For me, this is an incomparable loss to our society. What can equal the golden presence of gods and their incomparable exploits?

My Writing Life Begins

"YOUR FINAL ASSIGNMENT in this class will be the writing of a short story," Miss Bordewich said. "You will have two weeks to write it, and it will count for one half of your final grade."

The subdued moans from the senior English class could not stifle the excitement in her voice. Obviously, she was expecting prose on the level of Mark Twain and Bret Harte, whose short stories we had been studying.

I trailed behind my classmates as we left the room. A sixth sense must have given me a premonition of what was to come.

It came. My dragging feet could not postpone what was waiting for me in the guise of my high school sweetheart. She cuddled up to me as I walked with misgiving down the long hallway.

"I can't wait to see what you're going to write for me," she whispered conspiratorially.

"Don't wait too hard," I said. "I can't write your story."

June stopped short in her tracks and glared at me. If looks could kill, I was dead.

"What are you saying?" cried June. "I can't write a story, and you know it."

"I can't either," I said in helplessness. "I've never written a story."

"That's no excuse," cried June.

"The heck it isn't."

Tears welled up in her eyes. "Then what am I going to do? I'll flunk the class. Some boyfriend you are!"

What could I do? I was trapped as surely as one of Jack London's wolves. "Don't cry," I pleaded. "I'll try, but I'm not promising anything."

That was all she expected. The tears disappeared, and with a cheery wave, she was off down the hallway.

And try I did. Thinking up a story. Rejecting it.
Anticipating the kind of story Miss Bordewich
would expect from June, who was no honor student.
Creating characters, molding the girl to resemble
June. Choosing a boyfriend unlike me. Painting
golden sunsets and a couple walking hand in hand
into them. Fighting for every word and every sen-
tence to make them better.

When it was done, I typed it up on the Royal portable typewriter my mother had bought for themes
we brothers and sisters had to write.

Finally, the story was done, and I presented it to
June with love, one day before the deadline. I'm
not quite sure she even took the time to read it.
She clasped it to her breast and hurried off to turn
it in to Miss Bordewich, without a word of thanks
or the kiss I had expected, leaving me with the
dreadful realization that I had exactly one night to
write my own short story.

Somehow, I finished the story after midnight. It
had to do with a mystery and a detective, which is as
much of it as I can remember.

Convinced that it was an awful story, I sheepishly
handed it in to Miss Bordewich a few hours before

class time. She glanced at it and said not a word, leaving me with the suspicion that it would be I and not June who would flunk the course.

When class time came, I listened with disbelief as Miss Bordewich read my story to the class. I hung my head in embarrassment, refusing to look up or around. I could feel June's eyes boring into me from her seat in the back of the room.

As always, June was waiting for me in the hallway when class was done. She was almost apoplectic with rage. "You creep!" she cried in a very audible voice. "Do you know what grade she gave me for my short story? An F! I flunked the course, and it's your fault. You did it on purpose!"

She did not have to add, "Find yourself another girlfriend." But she did.

Homecoming

I STEPPED OFF the train onto the platform of the
Reno depot and looked expectantly for a familiar
face. It was night, and the depot was wet with rain. It
was also deserted, except for a soldier with a duffel
bag stepping onto the train down the way. I stood in
the rain for a while longer and then went into the
depot to wait for somebody to greet me.

My family had to know I was coming home after
a year overseas. The family home in Carson City was
probably closed, since my mother had rented an
apartment in San Francisco during the time we
brothers were scattered to the winds by World War II.

I had telephoned her from a phone booth in front of St. Patrick's Cathedral in New York when my ship had landed and disgorged its passengers. She had cried and I had cried. She had been incredulous, since there was no way I could have talked to her before leaving Africa.

She instructed me to go to the family home in Carson because she was going to leave San Francisco immediately and come home to Nevada to set up housekeeping.

After a short stop in Washington, D.C., resigning my post in the American Foreign Service and being debriefed by the State Department, I had gotten on the train for the four-day trip across the United States. Waiting in the depot, I had to surmise that she had not yet made the move home to Carson City.

From Washington, I had also sent a telegram to my father saying I was back in America and would be in Reno on a specific day in April. I sent the telegram with the vain hope that he might just leave his sheep in the hills and go to Carson for provisions and the mail.

The telegram had reached him, all right. I knew

that when I saw a tall, angular cowboy approaching me with clumping boots. He looked down at me and asked, "Are you Dominique Laxalt's son Robert?"

When I said yes, he said, "Well, he got word to me to pick you up and take you to his sheepcamp." I was saved. The mystery of where to go and how to get there was solved.

"Get your bag," the cowboy said. "You can spend the night with me in my room. I'm a roomer at the Star Hotel. That's a little Basque hotel down the street. You'll be on familiar ground, since you're a Basco, too."

The Basques who ran the hotel, providing rooms for sheepherders and cowboys in their time off, greeted me warmly. No going to bed without a hearty meal of soup and stew, french fries and a salad, and, of course, a glass of claret wine.

Since serving time at the long tables in the dining room was over, I ate in the kitchen, listening to the familiar tones of Basque by the owners and serving girls. My sense of abandonment disappeared, and I was feeling homecoming at last.

Next morning, the old cowboy and I set out for the range country where my father had his sheepcamp. With the rain, the sagebrush desert was fragrant and familiar.

We met and passed by my father's old stock truck on the highway. I let out a yell of recognition, and the old cowboy pulled his car to the side of the road. My father turned his truck around and joined us.

His first glimpse of me brought forth a moan of "Oh, my God, what happened to you?"

I grasped his work-hardened hand. "I'm all right now. I haven't had an attack of malaria since I left Africa. I've had a week at sea dodging submarines and a week in Washington and coming across country." Actually, I thought I looked pretty good. I had gained back a good five pounds out of the twenty-five I had lost in my siege with malaria and dysentery.

"I won't mention it again," my father said. "The important thing is you're alive and home."

We said good-bye and thanks to the old cowboy and went back the way my father had come. Twenty miles down the road, we left the highway and turned off on a two-lane dirt road. The jolting trip over rocks and sagebrush took me back to the days of growing up. When I sighted the triangular teepee tent that was my father's sheepcamp, the two sheep dogs started barking. I smelled the sagebrush cook fire from the tent, and then I really knew I was home again, at least in this part of my life. If my mother had made it back to Carson City, the whole part of homecoming would have been accomplished. As for now, the family home was still locked up and empty and would be for another few days. I would be living in the sheepcamp during that time.

My Uncle Pete was staying with my father, helping to herd the band of ewes and lambs grazing in the winter desert rangeland. Most of the winter's snow had melted, and there were only scattered patches of gleaming white remaining.

After the heavy moisture-laden jungle air I had been breathing, I could not get enough of the desert air. It was crystal clear and bright, the sky was a porcelain winter blue, and sagebrush, rock formations, and the snowcapped Sierra in the distance seemed to leap out at me.

That night, we ate dinner in the sheepcamp tent made of heavy canvas that kept the cold outside and the heat from the little tin woodstove inside. The glints of firelight from the chinks in the stove cast a golden glow over snow and sun-bronzed faces, utensils, and the ever-present Winchester carbine that hung on one of the tent poles.

Dinner was lamb chops, potatoes and onions, green peppers and garlic mixed in a Dutch oven. That and sourdough bread and wine in a tin cup surpassed any meal I had eaten in a long time. After dinner, I told them about my experiences in the troop ship that carried me across the ocean and the life I had led in Africa. I did not go into detail about the diseases I had gotten—malaria, yellow jaundice, amoebic dysentery, and the like. Their effects on me were, I knew now, evident enough without explanation. After dinner, I shared my father's bedroll with him.

So went the next few days, helping my father and my uncle herding sheep, getting acquainted with my land again, and regaining my health. I was sorry when it was done, but eager to go to my other home in Carson City. Enough time had passed to give my mother time to become installed in the family home.

The reunion in the family home had to be emotional. It was the first step in being together again. I embraced my mother and looked with surprise at how my sister Marie had grown into high school age and how my youngest brother Peter's voice was changing.

My journey was over. The war was nearing its end, and the future seemed predictable. My brother Paul would be coming home, his combat days behind him. My sister Suzanne, who had become a nun, was at least within telephone distance. The family home was filling with familiar voices and cooking scents. We were very nearly a united family again.

Fraternity Life

WORLD WAR II had ended, and university campuses were flooded with veterans whose expenses were paid by the government under the GI Bill. Many of them hardened by combat. The day of the pink-cheeked frosh was over.

It was to be a difficult time for fraternities with hallowed codes of conduct that called for such things as hazing and paddling.

My friend Pete and I had enrolled at the University of Nevada in Reno. Our first order of business had been to find a room we could rent in a house that took in students. That accomplished, we were

confronted with the problem of food. The only solution was to find a fraternity house that served
meals to its members. We tried three fraternities
under the subterfuge of considering membership.
Alpha Tau Omega was the hands-down choice. Its
cook was the best.

Dutifully, we and our fraternity brothers-to-be
went to the first initiation meeting. The frat president welcomed the new pledges in proper manner
and then recounted the history of the fraternity in
sacred tones. This should have given us a hint about
what was to come. He intoned the rules of conduct
expected of fraternity brothers and the penalties for
breaking the rules.

We new pledges thought he was kidding when he
laid down such laws as never walking on the green
quadrangle that was the showpiece heart of the old
campus. To go from one building to another without crossing the quad meant a long walk, which was
an irritation when there were classes to be met.

Chafee was a burly pledge who was one of the two
surviving members of the Malmédy massacre in
which German troops had shot American prisoners
of war. He made the mistake of laughing heartily

when the frat president said that the penalty for crossing the greensward of the quad was a severe paddling.

The frat president, white-faced with the committed sacrilege, ordered Chafee to come to the podium, or rather to the square in front of the podium. He then sent one of the pink-cheeked frat brothers to fetch a paddle the size of a tennis racket.

Paddle in hand, the president ordered Chafee to "assume the posture." When Chafee looked puzzled, the president told him to bend over, that his penalty for laughing was to be ten swats on his posterior.

Chafee regarded the president thoughtfully and then decided the president was serious. He asked the president if he could inspect the paddle. It was handed to him. Chafee tried it out on the palm of his hand, then, deliberately and without emotion, broke the paddle into pieces and handed them to the president, who almost fainted on the spot. He was supported by gasps from the other pink-cheeked pledges in the room.

So began our introduction into fraternity life. The aborted punishment was never spoken of again, and the codebook of rules was relegated to the wastepaper basket.

My roommate, Pete, and I almost scheduled a class for meeting nights. But it was not necessary. Chafee was elected president of the frat house, and his reign was marked with relaxation. He opened every meeting with an infectious, "Screw you, one and all."

Coping with Communism

COMMUNISTS WERE in short supply at conservative campuses such as the University of Nevada. The only student I knew of who proclaimed he was a Communist had transferred from the University of California at Berkeley, which was widely known as a hotbed of Reds, as they were then known.

The only reason I took the first class on Communism at Nevada was neither to show off nor to demonstrate that I was a rebel. In that time of old, worn-out subjects such as American history, I was genuinely intrigued. Everyone talked about Communism and the Red menace, but nobody knew anything about them. *Communism* was a bad word, and Communists were enemies. My schoolmates were certain I would emerge from the class as a flaming Red.

Of course, they were mistaken. The professor, Anatole Mazour, had been a White Russian opposed to Communism. He had escaped from Russia in what amounted to a slave ship. His purpose in teaching the workings of Communism was simply to show its flaws so that students would not be seduced into becoming Communist sympathizers.

Once the class started, I would not have dropped the course or skipped class for any reason. The czars whom we studied were murdered as regularly as clockwork, and I was not about to miss an assassination.

My friend and I did not refrain from telling our schoolmates what we were learning. We achieved something of a reputation as informed Communist haters. It was inevitable that our posturing would walk us into a confrontation with our campus Communist. He was an honest-to-goodness Communist, and he challenged my friend and me to a debate on the campus radio station. We readily accepted.

The first debate was a disaster. All our arguments were ground into the dirt. In desperation, we went to our Russian professor and asked him what we were doing wrong. He said, "Your Communist opponent is using false authority in his arguments. It is not unusual for Communists."

The professor did not have to add that we should do the same. We got the idea. In preparation for our next debate, we unearthed a wealth of false statements that we could attribute to Marx and Lenin.

When the debate came, we did not give our campus Communist a chance to prove us out. We lied glibly and mercilessly. His supercilious posture first wilted and then disintegrated. We won the debate hands down, and we were rewarded with a knowing smile from our Russian professor.

The Wolf Den

LIKE SMALL CAMPUSES everywhere, the University of Nevada had its favorite hangout.

Ours was the Wolf Den, situated across the street from the ornate, ivy-covered entrance to the campus. The Wolf Den, an invitingly shabby coffee shop badly in need of a coat of paint, shared its walls with the bookstore, also small and disorganized but somehow adequate to the needs of a student body of less than a thousand students.

For me and others like me who lived in rooming houses, the Wolf Den was the stop for early-morning coffee and a roll before eight o'clock classes.

On one particularly crisp day in autumn, I went into the Wolf Den wearing my trench coat with collar turned up against the chill. Students said I looked dramatic, and if the truth be told, that was the pose I was trying to affect. The requisite textbook and binder for my early-morning class went to fill out my bearing.

The Wolf Den was bustling with men students and co-eds, the men at the lunch counter and the co-eds crowded into wooden booths, their books balanced on their laps for want of space.

I found a seat at the end of the lunch counter and had my coffee and roll. My wristwatch said I had ten minutes to spare, so I indulged in a cigarette.

Directly behind me was a booth filled with co-eds I had vaguely noticed on my way down the line of jostling students.

When I was finished with my breakfast, I got down off my stool, ready to go out. In my haste, I bumped the books balanced on a girl's knees, tumbling them into the aisle. Mumbling an apology, I bent to pick up the books to return them to their owner. When I straightened up, I was looking into an elfin face with oblique eyes framed by long blond hair that reached her shoulders.

"I'm sorry," I managed to say.

"That's all right," the girl said in a firm voice that belied her fragile, sculpted features.

I stood transfixed for a long moment, then made my way down the aisle. If there is such a phenomenon as love at first sight, I was smitten at a first meeting of the eyes.

In a daze, I walked to my first class, a French class as it turned out, taught by a gentle old French professor with a graying moustache.

As the class filed in to take their seats, he motioned me back and asked in French if I spoke any French. I mumbled a few words of barbaric French mingled with the accents of African Swahili and Belgian.

Without making an issue out of it, he asked me if I had been in Africa. I nodded and went to find a seat.

Two co-eds seated in front of me were talking about sororities and teas. I was put off until one girl turned her head in profile. To my absolute surprise,

I recognized her as the girl in the Wolf Den whose books I had bumped.

That is all I remember of my first French class or, for that matter, the rest of my first day on campus. The girl told me later that she had spent her time staring down at the polished brown mosquito boots I had brought home from Africa. The semester that followed was one of hand-in-hand walks through a golden autumn, dream-filled dances in softly lighted halls, ice-skating in crisp autumn evenings, and cheek-chilling runs down Sierra ski slopes.

It all began with a single moment when there had been a bonding that would last a lifetime.

WRITING DAYS

Reporting Days

I MUST HAVE wanted to be a reporter badly if I was willing to hitchhike after news stories. But hitchhike I did, from Reno, where I was a student at the University of Nevada, to Carson City, which was the state capital and flourishing with unwritten news stories.

Though I had written high school sports stories for the sake of a by-line and a few dollars, I did not consider reporting my life's calling. I told myself that I was studying for the diplomatic service, ergo my courses in history, English, French, and sociology.

Since I was from Carson City, the city editor of the *Nevada State Journal* asked me to write a story about the appointment of a judge to the state supreme court. Of course I said yes, and then pored over a newspaper to find out how a news story was written. It seemed easy enough. I went to see the judge who had gotten the appointment, wrote my story, and was actually paid for it. I had found my life's calling, though I did not recognize it then.

More assignments came my way, since the *Journal* reporters were occupied with Reno stories. I had no car, so the only alternative was to walk to the city limits of Reno and hold out my thumb. To cover a multitude of high school football and basketball games, I merely walked to the field or gymnasium that sports editor Ty Cobb pointed me to.

By the time I graduated from the university, I was thoroughly entranced with the prospects of a reporter's life. I went back to Carson City and set up what I called the Capital News Service and went looking for clients. The *Reno Journal* was an automatic customer, as were several dailies throughout the state, the *Sacramento Bee* in California, and the United Press bureau in Reno.

My earnings were spare, so it was only natural that I would accept an appointment with United Press Associations.

I spent five years with United Press. Though the life was exciting, there were a few shortcomings—no overtime pay, no retirement prospects, and a small salary. But when one is young, none of these seem important.

The experiences were important. I covered disasters, politics, government on a state level, and—most important—the mob infiltration into Nevada gambling led by Benjamin "Bugsy" Siegel, one of the notorious bosses of the Bug and Meyer gang and an elite execution society known as Murder, Inc.

My First Gangster

EVERY YOUNG REPORTER dreams of his first scoop, as they called a big story then. I was a university student and a part-time reporter for the *Nevada State Journal* in Reno. There was a story in the *Reno Evening Gazette* about a shooting at a new luxury hotel called the Tahoe Village at Lake Tahoe. A man named L. M. Strauss was alleged to have shot a man named Harry Sherwood. No further details or identification.

When I saw that first story, I remembered something my kid brother, Peter, had told me. He was working as a caddy master at a golf course at Lake

Tahoe. He had been a little shaken up by the fact that one party of golfers was carrying pistols in their golf bags. Out of curiosity, he pored through some crime magazines to find out who they were.

He found one man's mug shot, Russian Louie Strauss, reputedly a member of Murder, Inc.

After the shooting, Strauss had been taken to Carson City and put in jail. I went to Carson City and talked the sheriff into letting me see Russian Louie, as Strauss was called. He was a tall, thin man with a long face and dead eyes, but he was affable enough.

Never having been in the presence of a real-life gangster, I was apprehensive. But when I asked him if he were indeed Russian Louie, he admitted it right out, with unmistakable pride. He went further than that. He said he was related to Charlie Fischetti, who had taken over the action in Chicago when Al Capone was sent to Alcatraz. I couldn't believe what I was hearing, but I decided to press my luck.

He told me that Harry Sherwood used to run the gambling ship *Lux* off of Los Angeles. Then he started reeling off the names of some of the people who were at Tahoe Village with him. Names like Abie "the Trigger" Chapman, George "the Professor" Kozloff, and Abe Barker. The names meant nothing to me, but they made very good copy for my news stories. To top it off, Strauss admitted he had shot Sherwood, but in self-defense. At that point, I made an astonishing discovery about gangsters. They weren't like their movie prototypes—brilliant minds that had taken a wrong turn and were poker-faced and tight-lipped. What occurred to me was that gangsters weren't smart at all. They just did things nobody else would do.

Later, when Sherwood died of his wounds, Russian Louie Strauss denied everything in court. The small-town district attorney who prosecuted him had never encountered Mafia-type witnesses before. Every man in the room where the shooting occurred, including Chapman and Kozloff, denied seeing a gun in Russian Louie's hands or witnessing the actual shooting. The case was dismissed for lack of evidence.

Though he won the legal end of it, Russian Louie was not as lucky with the Mafia end. He had incurred the implacable wrath of the crime bosses for his crude performance, and, worse, brought attention to the fact that organized crime had its tentacles in Lake Tahoe. He moved to Las Vegas, and one night two friends dropped by to pick him up for a pleasure drive to Los Angeles. Russian Louie departed, but he did not arrive. He was never seen again. Rumor had it that he was "planted" in the desert that Las Vegas wags describe as the archeologists' puzzle of the future, since it amounts to an unformalized but quite expansive graveyard.

The Purple Gang

THE REASON I could not believe what I was hearing was that I had been raised with the cinematic image of gangsters played by actors such as Edward G. Robinson and Jimmy Cagney. They were hard men who talked out of the side of their mouths, wore pinstriped suits and fedora hats. Their pastimes were robbing banks and shooting people with tommy guns.

So when Mert Wertheimer—a member of the Purple Gang out of Detroit—asked this young reporter if I wanted to hear how he had gotten kidnapped, I leaped at the chance.

Mert Wertheimer, who had moved to Reno and opened a gambling casino, looked the part of my gangster image. He was a gnomelike little man with a big head, cold eyes, and a rasping voice. His brother Louis was his partner in the gambling casino of the Riverside Hotel.

"It happened on a fishing trip to the Michigan Lakes," Mert said.

The idea of a gangster going fishing struck me as ridiculously funny, and I laughed.

"What's so funny?" Mert asked.

"I thought you were kidding me," I said.

"Well, I'm not kidding you," said Mert. "I'm a good fisherman. I even had a fishing cabin in the Michigan Lakes country. Spent a lot of time there."

I made my apologies, and Mert went on with his story. It seemed that it was a common practice in the Detroit underworld to "put the finger" on a gambler and set him up for kidnapping. It was a lucrative pastime, since gamblers had a lot of money.

"Anyway, I needed a vacation," said Mert. "So I asked Ruby Mathis to come with me and we took off."

That was good thinking, I thought to myself. Ruby

Mathis, who had come to Reno with Mert, had been described as a ruthless killer in a book about Murder, Inc., an organization that killed people on contract. What better security!

"Ruby and I were driving on the mountain road that led to my cabin," Mert said. "We came around a bend, and there was a car blocking the road. I stopped, and a couple of guys jumped out of the bushes with guns. One was Turkey Jack, who was a famous kidnapper in Detroit. When I saw him, I knew what was coming off. I had been fingered for a snatch."

Mert nodded sagaciously. "I was right. Turkey Jack was kidnapping me."

"What did Ruby do?" I asked. "Did he rub them out on the spot?"

Mert regarded me with disappointment. "What did Ruby do?" he repeated. "He fainted. Ruby never could stand the sight of a gun."

So much for the authenticity of the book on Murder, Inc., I told myself. To Mert, I said, "What happened then?"

Mert explained that when Ruby regained consciousness, Turkey Jack sent him back to Detroit to give Louis Wertheimer the news that his brother Mert had been kidnapped. He also named the ransom price. Ruby took Mert's car and headed back to Detroit.

"What did Turkey Jack do with you?" I asked.

"He drove me to my cabin, and we all settled down to wait for Ruby and the ransom money."

"Did Turkey Jack tie you up or beat you up?"

Mert shook his head as if he were about to give up on me.

"What did you guys do?" I asked.

"We played poker for two days," said Mert, "waiting for Ruby. I almost died."

I held my breath again. "Why? Did they think you had double-crossed them?"

"I almost died from their cooking," said Mert. "It gave me a bad case of indigestion. So I took over the cooking."

After another day, Ruby Mathis came back to the cabin. He did not come back with good news. He reported that Lou Wertheimer, Mert's brother, had refused to pay the ransom. Absolutely.

If Mert was disappointed, Turkey Jack was, too. He said to Mert, "I love you like a brother, Mert, even if you did clean me out in poker. That's not the point. I've got to kill you. For the good of the racket. You understand."

Mert told him, "I understand your position. But let me send Ruby back one last time."

"Turkey Jack said okay," said Mert. "So I had a little talk with Ruby Mathis. I told him to forget about getting the ransom money from Lou. I told him to go to Capone in Chicago. Al owed me a big one, and I was collecting."

Mert leaned back in his chair, signaling that the story was almost over. "Big Al came through. He got word to Turkey Jack to let me go free. Turkey Jack didn't like it very much, but when Al Capone ordered something done, it got done. So Turkey Jack left the cabin, and I finished my fishing vacation."

Something was missing from the story, and I asked about it. "Did you ever find out who put the finger on you to set you up for the kidnapping?"

"Oh, sure," Mert said. "It was my brother Lou."

"What did you say to Lou when you got back?" I asked Mert.

"Nothing. He's my brother, after all."

Executions

THE TREE-LINED ROAD of tall poplars was forbidding in the darkness before dawn, adding to my morbid state of mind. I was going to my first execution as a United Press correspondent.

I stopped at the armed entrance to the prison grounds and showed the guards my invitation, a black-rimmed card with the word *cordially* included, to demonstrate that the Nevada State Prison handled such occasions in a proper manner.

Parking my car and picking up my reporter's notebook, I joined the handful of men who had been invited to the execution. They consisted of a few state officials, dignitaries with a ghoulish set of mind, and reporters whose job it was to describe the execution.

We paused briefly in the waiting room and received our instructions and briefing on the conduct of the execution. Then, sliding steel doors began to open and we were led through them, following the maze to the inner prison yard. The lethal gas chamber was a small stone building not twelve feet square and brightly lighted in the dark courtyard. On the prison walls surrounding the yard, I could make out the patrolling guards outlined against the first pale daylight.

When we approached the gas chamber, we could see the condemned man. He was already strapped to a huge, obscene chair, thick leather straps binding his ankles, legs, chest, and arms to the chair. A stethoscope taped to his chest above his heart was attached to a tube that ran diagonally to the chamber wall and exited there to the doctor who was waiting outside.

Underneath the chair was a black vat filled with sulfuric acid. Dangling above it was a cluster of three pouches; each was tied to a separate cord that also protruded outside the chamber. The three pouches contained marbles, rocks, and cyanide pellets. Outside the chamber, the warden and two guards would each cut one cord, depositing the pouches into the vat of sulfuric acid. The cyanide pellets, when dropped into the vat, would release thick vapors of hydrocyanic gas that would flow upward around the condemned man's head. When he breathed the fumes, he would die.

The condemned man was a big man dressed in prison garb. His hair was tangled, and he appeared to be in a stupor. Still, he looked at each one of us as we gathered in front of the huge window that fronted the chamber.

The execution started without notice to any of the witnesses. Suddenly, thick wavy streams of hydrocyanic gas were pouring up from the vat. The condemned man looked down, startled, as if to find out where the vapors were coming from. Then he took his first breath. His face contorted as the fumes penetrated his nasal passages. His massive arms and legs and chest thrust mightily against the straps that bound him. For an instant, I thought the straps would break, freeing him. But the straps held fast, and after a few more breaths, he began to collapse.

We had been told that the condemned died instantly with the first breath, but it was not so. The man breathed stentoriously for five or ten minutes, growing weaker by the instant. Finally, his head collapsed on his chest, slobber pouring from his mouth and nose.

When the doctor removed the stethoscope from his ears, we knew the execution was over. The warden asked us to follow him out of the prison yard through the maze of steel gates into the waiting room. Nobody spoke, and we went out to our cars. I took notes. Every detail of the execution was indelibly stamped on my memory. It would turn into nightmares.

In the time that followed, I had to cover more executions, having no choice but to follow orders.

The one that troubled me most was truly bizarre. A young murderer, David Blackwell, hardly more than twenty-one, had shot and killed a Reno police officer. He was the son of a minister in the state of Washington. He fled to Nevada after killing one of his own kind. He was traced to a small hotel on Sierra Street with an accomplice. When the police burst through the door, he was sitting in bed with a revolver hidden beneath the sheets. When the officer threw back the sheets, Blackwell unveiled his pistol and killed the officer. In the gunfight that followed, Blackwell was wounded by another police- man, but not seriously. Before he was taken from the room on a stretcher, the policeman who had shot him told him, "The next time you see me, I will be watching you die in the prison's gas cham- ber."

On the morning of the execution, the policeman was standing against the window directly in front of Blackwell. When the execution began, the police- man was going to press a badge against the window so that it would be the last thing Blackwell saw.

When the hydrocyanic gas was released, it came up in waves around Blackwell's head. Instead of showing agony or fear, however, Blackwell looked at the policeman. His lips formed a "Whew!" and he smiled. The policeman kept the badge in his pocket. He said to me, "What a football player he would have made."

Transition

TO BE TWENTY-NINE years old and jobless is not funny. It is even less funny when one is newly married, has a child, and has bought a house.

My time as a staff correspondent for United Press was done after five years. There is a tradition of impermanence with wire services. Correspondents can expect to stay with one bureau five years or less. I was given the choice of being the bureau manager in Mexico City, which I did not want, or an alternative choice of becoming the news chief at the United Press bureau in Los Angeles, which I also did not want. I had gotten married, my wife and I had an infant son, and we had bought a house. Further, I was a Nevadan to the core and could not see raising a family in either Mexico or Los Angeles. So I had no choice but to resign.

I did not anticipate any difficulty in finding another new reporting job. In my five years at United Press, I had just about covered the waterfront—politics, the legislature, murders and executions, and the workings of state government. To my surprise and anger, none of these accomplishments seemed to matter. The only thing that counted was that there were no openings anywhere. All the news media—newspapers or radio or the new public relations field—were staffed up. I found out what it was to pound the streets looking for a job, and for the first time, I knew panic.

Then an opening materialized. The University of Nevada in Reno wanted to create a news service and publications office. All my credentials were in place. However, the new president of the university, Minard Stout, was locked into a death struggle with his faculty over the firing of three professors who had challenged his policy of "professional educators." In my interview, I made the mistake of saying that I wanted no involvement in the controversy. That was enough for the president to turn me down for the news service job.

I had gotten to know some members of the Board of Regents of the university well, and I went to them to appeal my case. By some miracle, they chose to side with me and I won the job. My position in the academic freedom controversy was not mentioned, and I was not about to bring it up.

I worked very hard to prove myself, often working nights after a grueling day of news writing. My wife, Joyce, became a schoolteacher and taught French for eighteen years. The regents and the new president were pleased, and my life seemed to be on a positive track again. The mortgage could be paid, and although newsmen's salaries are notoriously low, we could at least pay the grocery bills.

I had served under three presidents—Minard Stout, who was fired by the Regents; Charles J. Armstrong, a classicist; and William R. Wood. Armstrong was just what the university needed then, and he was a supporter of initiating a university press in Nevada.

My news service office had become one of multiple functions—news stories about administration, faculty, and students; alumni relations; and athletics. When the new vice president, William R. Wood, suggested that a university press should be considered, I leaped at the opportunity.

Methodically, I began shedding the multiple functions of the news service office and concentrating on founding a university press to publish faculty works. From my own writing, I knew about the writer's function, but I knew nothing about the practical side of book publishing. I set about to learn what I should know by talking to publishers from universities that had operating presses and publishing programs. The results of my interviews were mixed. Stanford University said, "That's all we need, another university press." The dean of university press publishing, Savoie Lottinville of the University of Oklahoma Press, consented to come to Reno and talk to university powers-that-be about the pros and cons of university press publishing. He convinced the Board of Regents that Nevada should enter the field. There were huge gaps to be filled in such fields as Nevada history. Lloyd Lyman, then the assistant director of the University of California

Press, volunteered to guide us through the many pitfalls of publishing—a wonderful gesture. The Regents and the administration at Nevada said, "Go ahead." The only obstacle was the essential one—money. Having no success in providing private financing, I went to the legislature. The chairman of the Senate Finance Committee, the key source of all appropriations, actually authorized enough money for our first book—seventy-five hundred dollars. Small as the appropriation was, it was at least a start.

As time went by, the situation improved. I was given authorization and money to hire someone who knew publishing from the manuscript perspective. Lloyd Lyman rode herd on our aspiring program. He was the godfather who told us where not to make mistakes, what to publish, and how to organize a press operation. Without him, there would never have been a University of Nevada Press.

Meanwhile, the multiple functions of my news service job began to be distributed elsewhere—catalog publishing, alumni relations, sports publicity, and so on. It took years, but finally a University of Nevada Press, complete with lean but competent staffing, was in place. I personally took on the task

of raising money, and happily, it began to material-
ize. The Max C. Fleischman Foundation gave us a
half-million dollars. An editorial board was named
to pass on manuscripts—most of which emanated
from the faculties at UNR and UNLV. To help with
raising funds, I formed a citizens' group, the
Friends of the University Press, which operated with
reasonable success. The publishing program began
to carry its own weight, the university paid staff salaries, and we were beginning to attract attention. The
hundred details of a university-press publishing
program fell into place, and the University of Nevada Press was launched.

On the Road with *National Geographic*

MY TOUR OF DUTY as a contract writer for the National Geographic Society began at a meeting between Jim Cerutti, an editor for the magazine, and my agent, Emilie Jacobson of Curtis Brown, Ltd.

It seemed that *National Geographic* wanted to do a story on Basque sheepherders of the American West. The magazine routinely assigned a writer and a freelance photographer to do the story. The photographer, William Belknap, had covered his end of the assignment, and *Geographic* had an adequate supply of photographs in hand. But the writer, an eastern product on his first venture into the western hinterland, had written an unacceptable story. *Geographic* then assigned a southern writer to do the story, but he was more out of his element than the eastern writer was. The story did not pass muster with *Geographic*'s editors.

As Jim Cerutti dolefully told Emilie Jacobson, the magazine was out a lot of money and the story was in limbo. Emilie Jacobson asked Cerutti if he had read a book called *Sweet Promised Land* by Robert Laxalt. Cerutti said no, and Emilie promised to send him a copy. She did so; Cerutti read the book— the story of my father's life as a sheepherder—and phoned me with the assignment. As a beginning writer, I accepted heartily. Cerutti sent me a guide to writing a story for *Geographic,* which amounted to a few thousand words of do's and don'ts.

I followed my directions scrupulously and sent in the story. Cerutti said the story did not have the same warm feeling as my book. I told him I wasn't asked to write the kind of story they wanted. Cerutti said, "Oh, write it your own way." Which I did, and the story was accepted.

That episode was to launch a relationship that went on for a number of years, about twenty in all, and that produced many magazine stories and book chapters for the National Geographic Society.

It also opened the door to any number of strange experiences that were not included in the stories and book chapters.

For example:

On a state story about New Mexico, I came upon a chapel called El Santuario at Chimayó, in the Sangre de Cristo Mountains. The chapel contained a hole in the ground whose earth was said to have healing powers. Pilgrims had been coming to El Santuario for many years to take away some of the sacred earth in the hole. I questioned the little priest who was pastor of the chapel, and he told me the legend of El Santuario's healing powers. He also confirmed local legend that despite many years of earth being taken from the hole, the hole remained the same size. Dutifully, I included this legend in my story.

When an informant has been quoted in a story, *National Geographic* policy requires that the source of the quote verify it. *National Geographic* did. The little priest had to confess that the hole did not retain its size by some miracle. He said that the reason the

hole grew no larger was because he would periodically fill it with dirt hauled to the chapel in a wheel-
barrow under cover of night. Of course, he told
Geographic, he would not like that part of the legend
included in the story, because it would disillusion
many hundreds of the faithful. *National Geographic*
asked me for my guidance. I promptly answered,
"Let's drop the quote. I have no desire to offend
Mother Church."

National Geographic stories for contract writers come
about in two ways: as assignments by *Geographic* editors or as suggestions from the author. The latter
course is rare, since the chances of an untested
writer receiving an assignment is, as one editor
wrote, "a thousand to one." Staff editors at *National
Geographic* in Washington, D.C., write the choice stories.

Once a contract writer receives an assignment to
do a story on anything ranging from the size of the
universe to a rare insect, he is expected to do at least
a month of research on his topic. Then he is sent on
a field trip for a month to six weeks, viewing sites,
interviewing people, and so on. When he comes
home, he is given a month to write his story. It is

then subjected to the scrutiny of *Geographic* editors in Washington. The story is then sent back to the writer for rewrite based on editors' criticisms. The story then goes back to staff editors for approval or rejection. If the story is approved, the uninitiated writer falsely assumes that his work is done. Actually, it is just beginning.

To quote from a *New York Times* story about *National Geographic*: "Built into the editorial process at *National Geographic* is an unusual fact-checking cadre, the *researchers.* They do their work after the stories have been written and try to demolish facts and assumptions of the writers so that the end product conforms to the *Geographic*'s rubric of absolute accuracy."

"They begin with the assumption," says assistant editor Joseph Judge, "that the writer is a *liar* and doesn't know what he's talking about."

Researchers send copies of quotations to people quoted in their stories. They seek third-party opinions and occasionally visit distant lands already visited by the writers.

"Those same writers expect such scrutiny and collect evidence from all over the Earth. One even brought back dried camel dung to the *Geographic* to prove it didn't smell. Another fried eggs for *Geographic* in a golden frying pan to prove gold had good conductivity."

My own classic encounter with Research came about in this way: I had written a paragraph saying, "On a late winter's day in 1539, explorer priest Fray Marcos de Niza looked down from a mountain and saw in the distance what he believed to be the fabled city of Cibola." A woman editor from *Geographic* phoned me and said: "We have been back to de Niza's journals. Although there was snow on the ground, we are unsure whether we can truly say it was winter or classify his vantage point as a mountain."

I said airily in response, "Let's just say: On a day between winter and spring in 1539, Fray Marcos de Niza looked down from a high hill." Research's response, to say the least, was explosive. The editor said, "I've had four researchers working for a week on that passage, and you are trying to dismiss our efforts with poetic license."

The encounter ended in a draw with, "On a spring day in 1539" and "looked down from a height. . . ."

My most harrowing assignment for *National Geographic* was a descent into the Grand Canyon by muleback. Since I suffer from acrophobia, I had qualms about accepting this assignment. Turning down an assignment is risky business when dealing with *National Geographic,* so I consented to take the story on.

The first time I looked down into the Grand Canyon was a terrifying experience, but I could not withdraw from the ordeal. As if my predicament were not bad enough already, an April blizzard came out of the north and blanketed me, my mule, and the awful edge of the canyon. Half of the riders scheduled to go on the trip canceled out with the first snowflake, being wiser than I. The rest of us, guided by trusty Arizona wranglers, decided to go through with the adventure.

One by one, we began the descent down the Bright Angel Trail, a narrow dirt path covered with snow. I had never known that mules skied before, but I learned it now. Slipping and sliding, we skirted the edge of the chasm in something resembling a slalom. In one sense, I was grateful for the blizzard, because it obscured the awful depths. But

as we worked our way deeper into the canyon, the warmer climes turned the snowflakes into rain and exposed the canyon depths a thousand feet below.

To keep from looking down at the depths, I decided to make a study of mules' ears, when they were cocked forward and why and when they were laid back to listen for the progress of the mules at the rear of the train.

By that time, I was drenched through, and there was nothing I could do about it except to think about something else.

The something else was not far in the offing. The Grand Canyon is covered with loose dirt that occasionally breaks loose in a small avalanche, particularly during rainstorms. The wrangler in front of me was caught in one of these minor avalanches, unloosing a boulder that swept away his mule's footing. Both mule and rider slid off the trail. The edge of the chasm was no more than fifty feet away, and I had a nightmarish premonition of watching both mule and man being swept over the edge.

In a lifesaving maneuver, the wrangler shoved himself off the saddle and clutched at a fortunately located bush that could hold his weight. He was saved, and my next premonition was of seeing the fallen mule glide over the edge to his death. But instinct saved him. He took one look over the edge and scrambled to stay on the slope. Somehow, he was successful, and the valiant wrangler slid down to grasp the mule's reins and pull him back to the remnant of trail we had been descending. The mule was a quivering, bloody mess of an equine when he finally made it back to the trail, but the patient wrangler stroked him until his nerves had settled. The wrangler could do nothing about the cuts and bruises on his mule. They would have to wait until we reached the station at the bottom of the canyon.

Compared to the fate of a pack mule at the end of the train, the mule I have been writing about was fortunate. The pack mule was apparently nearsighted, and thirsty. To alleviate his thirst, he stepped off the trail to get a drink of water from a creek he noticed was flanking the trail. The creek happened to be the Colorado River one thousand feet below. The wranglers felt sorrow and a sense of loss at the incident. Not for the pack mule, but for what he was packing—a week's supply of Coors beer.

Spine of the Pyrenees

"WE WANT YOU to follow the spine of the Pyrenees Mountains from the Atlantic Ocean to the Mediterranean and tell us what you find there."

So went the assignment from *National Geographic* magazine.

When one becomes a contract writer for *National Geographic,* he can expect a variety of assignments such as this, and the experiences that go with them. In my time, I had:

Probed the hidden corners of the Lost Sierra, held in the palm of my hand a golden nugget freshly

found in a creek, and known the fever that had triggered the California Gold Rush of '49.

I had huddled in an adobe chapel in the Sangre
de Cristo Mountains of New Mexico on a Good Fri-
day midnight, knowing that in a *morada* nearby a man
was being crucified.

I had broken bread with a Basque sheepherder in
his lonely camp.

I had undergone the ordeal of a five-day horseback trip through cactus and rattlesnake country in
the Superstition Wilderness of Arizona.

And I had traveled by horseback, jeep, and on
foot, tracing the California Trail that the gold-
seeking Forty-Niners took.

I wasn't sure what I would find on the sinuous
mountain roads that went for 270 miles from one
end of the Pyrenean chain to the other, traversing
forty peaks exceeding 10,000 feet.

I was not disappointed. In Biarritz, the beginning
of my assignment, I found the grand hotels that
Empress Eugénie, Napoléon III, Queen Victoria,
and Bismarck had frequented to make the town the
"queen of resorts."

In the French National Park, I was to see what French author Victor Hugo had called "the Colosseum of Nature"—the Cirque de Gavarnie— a two-mile-wide bowl with walls rising up a mile from the valley floor, a gouged amphitheater that is breathtaking in its beauty.

I saw the Principality of Andorra, which Napoléon wanted to make into a museum piece. Sadly, however, Andorra's modest import duties and bargain prices for radios, cameras, and even Brazilian cigars have made Andorra a tourist magnet whose new riches are causing the demolition of antiquity.

In Pamplona, made famous by Ernest Hemingway's *The Sun Also Rises*, we witnessed the running of the bulls through village streets and, of course, the classic bullfight that followed.

In Tiermas, we found an almost-deserted medieval town with only a handful of residents too old to move.

In Lourdes, that world-known shrine where thousands of the crippled and the sick have claimed cures, I stood in the grotto where Bernadette was said to have witnessed the Blessed Virgin.

Geographic had instructed me to tell them "what you find there along the spine of the Pyrenees."

They were satisfied.

The Gauchos

A son am I of the rolling plain
A gaucho born and bred . . .
And this is my pride: to live as free
As the bird that cleaves the sky.

THIS WAS THE REFRAIN that was going through
my mind as a molten sun was rising off the horizon
of the seemingly endless pampa of Argentina. The
gauchos passed like shadows across its face and vanished into the mist, like phantoms of all their forebears who had ridden onto the rolling plain.

Victor Carrillo, the ranch manager, my wife,

Joyce, and I followed at a trot. The sun was burning off the mist to reveal a sparkling winter morning. Black-and-white lapwings swooped over our heads. Hawks perched on fence posts, and tiny white-collared owls eyed us gravely from the tall grass. Ostrichlike rheas fled with springy, high-stepping strides at our approach.

So began what was probably the most exotic assignment I would undertake for *National Geographic* magazine.

In the weeks that followed, I learned the life of the gauchos. It is one of the few genuine horse cultures left in the world. From cradle to grave, the horse is the center of their existence. They learn to ride almost as early as they learn to walk. Most will pass their lives never having ridden in a motorized vehicle. They live in adobe huts scattered across the sea of grass that is known as the legendary pampa, tending cattle for ranches or *estancias* that once encompassed 260,000 acres of grassland. Most are descended from outlaws who were exiled from such metropolitan centers as Buenos Aires. In the early 1800s, two things happened to transform the gaucho from outlaw to hero. Argentina decided to throw off the yoke of Spanish colonization, and military leaders saw in the gauchos the potential of a ferocious mounted guerrilla force. They served in the War of Independence, pitiless in battle, indifferent to suffering, and with huge powers of endurance. All they needed to survive were a horse, a knife, and a lance.

In the time that followed, the immense pampa was broken into ranches that raised cattle for beef and leather, and the gaucho became the equivalent of an American working cowboy.

This was the story I sought in my *National Geographic* assignment that took me to the far corners of the ocean of grass.

Oddly enough, the gaucho assignment had a goodly part of its origin in Reno. In Washington, D.C., *National Geographic* editors were having trouble finding a writer to tackle a sweeping story such as the gauchos posed. The problems of the story were imposing, mostly having to do with sources for story material.

Coincidentally, an elderly woman, Mary Etta Kleberg of the King Ranch's founding family, one of the heirs to the King Ranch, the most far-spread ranching operation in the world, had moved to Reno. After reading my first national book, *Sweet Promised Land,* she wanted to meet me. While we talked, I told her about the gaucho assignment I had accepted, with doubts. She informed me that the King Ranch syndicate owned a huge ranching operation in Argentina and offered help, which I quickly accepted. She made the necessary arrangements that turned the assignment into a success instead of a floundering failure.

In the first place, the Argentine government was not at all sympathetic to my needs. In fact, Argentina and the United States had broken off relations. In the second place, my brother Paul was a U.S. senator, and the Argentineans seemed determined to believe that I was on an intelligence mission and the gaucho story was a subterfuge. Last, the government posted an armed guard outside our hotel room for our entire stay and added someone to follow us wherever we went. He was an amateur, but the .45 automatic that showed through his suit was very professional. On the day we arrived, we were summoned at night to a stone fortress and a dungeon room for questioning. When our interrogators decided I might be legitimate, they showed a film boasting Argentine potentials and wonders. Tired, I went to sleep during the showing, which further proved my innocence.

Inflation was rampant, running to 130 percent. On the day we arrived, two hamburgers and tea cost $50. For cocktails, vodka and brandy were out of the question, priced at $50 a drink. We settled for sherry at $79 a bottle. Happily, *National Geographic* pays all expenses.

Having made our King Ranch contact, everything changed for the better. We were flown by private plane to the King Ranch, one thousand miles into the interior, housed in an attractive cottage, and offered everything we needed in the way of guides. Most important, we were in the land of the legitimate gaucho that I have mentioned, a horse culture with remarkable sources of information—men and women whose families had been in Argentina since Spanish colonial days.

On our return, two young government agents—obviously irritated at our elusive escape into the interior—were there with a badly concealed tape recorder to interrogate me. With ill-concealed glee,

I told them more than they would ever want to know about gauchos.

Still, the constant government surveillance was harrowing. After all, several thousand academics, writers, and dissidents had disappeared. *Reader's Digest* reported later that they were flown out over the Pacific and thrown out of airplanes.

So it was with relief that we left Argentina safe and sound. To celebrate our departure, once we were airborne I ordered two vodka tonics and caviar and vowed to kiss the good American earth when we arrived in Miami. *National Geographic*'s reaction was, "Thank God you're safe, we were worried about you." I thanked them with bad grace.

Latter-Day Innocents Abroad

THE YEAR WAS 1960. My wife and I had decided that a stay in France was important to my writing career. The decision was made with the vaguest of notions as to what the future held.

Perhaps this uncertainty was the reason we decided to take America with us in no less than thirteen suitcases and two trunks. They contained clothes for all seasons for two adults and three children, our family silver, ball dresses and hats for Joyce and the gay Parisian life she anticipated, and, last but not least, an electric blanket.

Our luggage was to become the bane of our existence as we shuttled it from home to airport to a New York taxi to a New York hotel, and finally to the hold of the SS *Rotterdam,* there to rest unseen until we docked at Le Havre.

The junket from Le Havre to Paris opened up the luggage nightmare again. After our fifteen pieces of luggage had been jammed and tied onto a pint-sized French taxicab, there was little room left for passengers.

The French cab deposited us at the Hotel de Paris, shrugging aside my protests about price gouging with a Gallic, "La vie est chère."

Somehow, all fifteen pieces and five passengers managed to fit into the Volkswagen bus I had pre-purchased from America.

To get the VW pointed toward our destination in the South of France was another problem. There was no way I was going to risk our lives trying to cope with the mad swirl of traffic around the Arc de Triomphe. I was not alone in my faintheartedness. An American standing beside me on the curb said, "I come from Los Angeles and I can handle the freeway traffic there, but I am not going to throw my life away in that maelstrom."

That decided me. I hired a driver to take us to the Paris city limits.

Abodes

MANY YOUNG AMERICAN writers, their imaginations fired by memories of Paris's Lost Generation, yearn to live and write in a French village. They take it for granted that every village is fully stocked with clean, inexpensive cottages for the taking.

Sadly, such is not the case.

As we were to learn, there are no cottages for rent. They are already occupied by the village's residents.

Our first venture in finding a place to live—any

place—was in the fishing village of Saint-Jean-de-Luz on the Bay of Biscay.

Fruitless in our efforts to find a cottage, we were forced to settle for a villa, no less. The cozy abode we had searched for was now a three-story French summer villa with a spacious living room, a dining room, one story of bedrooms for Joyce and me and our three children, and one story of maids' quarters which, save one, remained unoccupied.

When word got around town that the summer villa—called *Mati Baita* or *Marie lives here*—was being occupied for the autumn by Americans (who are always rich), there was a land rush of maids in starched black attire at our door.

We settled for a fisherman's widow who could help Joyce with the housework and cooking. She also pointed Joyce toward the best shops and stalls for vegetables, fruit, and meat on a merchants' street called Rue Gambetta.

We passed autumn and the beginning of winter at an exorbitant price for our checkbook, braving the furious tempests of the Bay of Biscay. Raincoats were *obligé* on most days.

Which leads me to the subject of clothes. The American clothes we had brought simply were not acceptable. Bruce was tormented by his playmates until he socked their leader. Joyce provided a more acceptable solution to Bruce's clothing dilemma by driving him to Bayonne, a nearby commercial town. Bruce went to school the next day dressed in the acceptable turtleneck sweater and tight-fitting *fusée* pants. His dilemma was solved.

Between the second and third trimester, we moved from the coast to the mountains, to Saint-Jean-Pied-de-Port, once the fortified capital of Navarre.

Wanting to know how the Basques lived a century ago, I convinced Joyce that we should rent a run-down villa inhabited in part by a landlady who kept ducking in and out of a trapdoor that led to her quarters.

It was winter, the villa was cold and bare, and kitchen facilities were primitive. The only heat was from a lone fireplace. The villa cynically was named *Esker Ona,* meaning *Good Thanks* in Basque. We promptly renamed it *No Thanks* and went looking for another abode.

With luck, we found a reasonably clean little villa near the tracks of the narrow-gauge rickety railroad. It was called *La Nina.*

La Nina served us well. It was centrally located, giving Joyce access to shops housing the butcher, baker, and candlestick maker. The children went to school in the Citadel built by Napoléon on the top of a hill overlooking the ramparts of the fortified village. And I had an attic room that passed for a study where I wrote. My allegorical novel, *A Man in the Wheatfield,* was born in that attic room. *La Nina* was also near the village market, where I was to gather valuable notes for my writing.

The villa had a family of its own, household flies that hovered over our dinners but did not descend until dinner was over. They had obviously been trained in proper fly behavior.

In the beginning, at Saint-Jean-de-Luz, the language barrier was a formidable one for us and for our three children. The claim that English was a universal language was a myth in Basque villages.

Joyce had a thorough grounding in reading and writing French, but not in the spoken language. My French was a doubtful product of college French and idiomatic Swahili French learned in the Belgian Congo. The children knew French songs taught to them by Joyce in their infancy.

Lack of spoken French weighed most heavily on Bruce, age nine, Monique, age seven, and Kristin, age four. None of their teachers or schoolmates spoke English, and school subjects were taught in French. Their lamentations bore heavily on me, and I was convinced they were being traumatized by culture shock.

What I like to believe is that American spirit won out in the end—that and the fact that children have the gift of imitation. In one month, all three of our offspring were speaking French fluently. Not scholarly French, but the French that would enable them to cope in school and on the playground. Before the autumn semester was over, Bruce was awarded the *Prix d'Honneur* by his teachers.

My lacking in French actually worked to my benefit. At village feast days, men would sit around a table, drink red wine, and talk about their lives. They felt superior and sorry for me, and they felt free to *raconter* their lives in front of me. When the feast day was over, I had added materially to my storehouse of notes.

Joyce by now had little problem with spoken French. Once the dam was broken, she spoke fluent and correct French in her dealings with school officialdom and shopkeepers and family. As for me, I moved from present-tense French to past and, hesitantly, future tenses. I even learned a subjunctive that served to impress my listener. It was "*quoi qu'il en soit*"—"be that as it may."

Five years later, on our second sojourn in France we fared much more easily. Language was no problem, the children's garb was acceptable, and we were accustomed to French ways.

Our fourth abode was actually a cottage, loaned to us rent-free by my cousin's wife, a French lawyer and magistrate. It was located in Arcachon on the Atlantic seaboard, the oyster capital of France. It was inevitable that we would become impassioned with oysters in their own brine, sourdough bread, and chicken soup for suppers.

The cottage—named *Bizi Gochua,* "The Good Life" in Basque—was a summer cottage hardly equipped for seaboard winters. For a while, a fireplace was our only real heating. Then our generous landlady brought us an electric steam heater, which solved our problems, at least for the living room, dining room, and kitchen. Downstairs, where we slept and I wrote, was another matter.

Joyce's and my bedroom became my working space. Each morning, after coffee, I would bundle up, grit my teeth, and descend into the arctic depths.

Warming my fingers over the steam rising from my coffee cup proved unsatisfactory, so Joyce improvised a solution. She bought a pair of flannel gloves and cut off the fingers half-length. That solved my problem, except for the days when the cold froze my typewriter keys.

Our evenings in the living room were cozy and busy. Joyce would help our daughters, Monique and Kristin, with their French studies. Bruce sat in a corner, his little desk illuminated by a candle when the frequent tempests brought power failures, pronouncing his English assignment. His command of American English was penalized. The proper pro-

nunciation was English spoken in the British manner.

When Christmas came, Joyce had an inspiration.
Instead of the barren French Christmas, she would
put on an Anglo-Saxon Christmas for our relatives,
who would come from Bordeaux.

The entire family joined in the effort. From a
nearby forest, I poached a little pine tree, and Joyce
gathered an armful of holly, out of which she fash-
ioned a wreath of leaves and berries. This was attached to the front door in Anglo-Saxon greeting.

The children provided the ornaments—chains of
paper figures out of Christmas lore—to be draped
over our pine branches.

Our youngest, Kristin, practiced the words to
"La Petite Chèvre de Monsieur Seguin," which
would provide the floor show before Christmas dinner.

Joyce performed miracles in her preparations for
an American Christmas dinner. She found a tender
hen turkey at a poultry store. The cranberries were
actually brought from the United States. Joyce had
anticipated their absence from French grocery store

shelves. Apple and pumpkin pies would be dessert.

The dining room was ready, the table was set. All was in readiness for an Anglo-Saxon Christmas.

The family contingent from Bordeaux was somewhat taken aback by what met their eyes. The party included my two aunts—my mother's sisters, Aurélie and Claire—Claire's husband, Maurice, sons Peyo and Jean, and daughter Michèlle.

They all pretended to happy astonishment, but my Aunt Aurélie, sensitive to such things, was genuinely charmed.

Whatever doubts my young cousins had about an *American* feast were dispelled with the meal. All ate happily and well, and sipped good French wine.

After dinner, everybody retired to the living room for a proper period of gestation. Everyone, that is, except my two male cousins. They had hardly found a seat when I crooked a finger at them and said, "Come hither."

They came reluctantly, but they came. I led them into the kitchen, confronted them with a mountain of dishes, and said, "In America, the guests do the dishes."

Typical French youths who had never shared in

the housework, they were appalled. But I was adamant, and finally they shed their jackets and got to work. My aunts were delighted, Uncle Maurice doubtful.

Despite the rude shock to my cousins' systems, the Christmas dinner *à la Américaine* was a stunning success. But I seriously doubt whether the custom will be perpetuated.

OUR FIFTH AND FINAL abode made up for all the shortcomings of the ones that went before.

It was a modest villa that lay in the outskirts of Saint-Jean-Pied-de-Port. Designed in Basque architecture, it was built of white plaster with red trim. There was a spacious bedroom for Joyce and me, another for son Bruce, another for daughters Monique and Kristin, and, of all things, a guest room. The living room had a modern fireplace, the kitchen was equipped with a gas stove and refrigerator, and the dining room had a chandelier. My study boasted an ample desk and French doors, so that I could look up from my writing and watch and listen to the frequent, lulling rain showers.

More house makes for more visitors. From the

onset of our occupancy, there was a steady stream of houseguests, mostly from the United States.

Two were college graduates who brought laughter and good spirits to the household with their accounts of stealing. Their prey was wooden cow collars and village flags along their way. One theft in particular was high on the list of escapades—scaling a wall and making off with a flag from an edifice called the *Hôtel de Ville,* which they took to be a hotel, but it wasn't. When we told them that the building was the mayoralty, they were subdued, but only temporarily.

Jon Mirande was a Basque scholar, poet, and linguist, and my distant cousin. He helped me in appraising the value of the Library of Congress holdings in Basque studies. As we leafed through a copy of the Library's card file, I was to learn that he had read every one of the books in French, Spanish, German, Russian, English, and, of course, Basque. He could pronounce judgment on every book, weighing its contribution to Basque history and culture, and listing its demerits if a book did not prove up in his standards.

Jon Mirande had a few other attributes. He was clairvoyant and a mind reader. He would respond to a question before I asked it. In the beginning, this unnerved me a little, but after a while, I realized that it was giving me a sense of peace. I knew I could never lie to him, or exaggerate my knowledge of what we were talking about.

Another of Jon Mirande's attributes did unsettle Joyce, however. When Mirande began revealing himself, we learned that he had consort with the *laminak,* the "little people" of Basque mythology, and the *basa jaun,* the Basque god of the forest. He also prayed for the conversion of the Pope to Christianity.

That he was also a poet of some repute we were not to learn until later. His verse was regarded as scandalous and anticlerical.

Jon Mirande committed suicide on a Christmas Eve—in protest against the holy Catholic Church.

I was not surprised. He at least had added a touch of the occult and macabre to our French experience. That in part asked for forgiveness for his heretic ways.

SELECTED BOOKS
AND HOW THEY CAME TO BE

Genesis of *Sweet Promised Land*

SWEET PROMISED LAND was my first national book and certainly the most long lasting, forty years now in print. If one is ever really remembered for anything, I guess this will be it for me.

I can't pronounce dictums or get too analytical about this book or anything else I've written, because the creative process is largely unexplainable. Ernest Hemingway said it right when he told George Plimpton in that remarkable *Paris Review* interview that a writer must never talk about the fragile part of his story while he is writing it—the fragile part being the real story beneath the story, that intangible something that a writer is hard put to explain to himself.

Sweet Promised Land is a memoir of my father's return to the Basque Country of his birth in France after half a century on the mountain and desert ranges of the American West. He came to this country in 1906. He was sixteen or eighteen years old, we don't know which. At various times in his life, he was a ranch hand in the Smoke Creek Desert of northern Nevada. He was a mustanger, a horse breaker, a sheepherder, and a livestock baron of sorts, owning at one time about sixty thousand head of sheep, five thousand head of cattle, a few hundred good saddlehorses, ten ranches, and hundreds of miles of rangeland in Nevada and California.

He went almost broke in the farm and ranch crash of the early 1920s. After his last two thousand head of sheep and lambs froze to death in the northern deserts, he hit the road working at anything having to do with livestock. He worked as a ranch hand again. He herded sheep. He cowboyed. Slowly, he built his way back up to five thousand sheep or so and effectively ended his life as a working sheepherder when he sold his outfit. It had become clear to him that none of his four sons would follow him in the sheep business.

This varied life of his actually posed my first problem. Which pursuit should I choose to write about, to begin with, to emphasize? Not so obviously, it came down to the fact that he was a sheepherder for most of his life.

My accompanying him on his journey home to the Pyrenees Mountains that hold the Basque Country came about this way:

Since modern times had passed my father by, I was delegated by the family to accompany him and guide him through the maze of airports and big cities we would encounter. Also, I was to make sure not only that he got there, but also that he came back. My mother was convinced that once he got back to where he came from, we would never see him again.

Finally, I was just plain curious to see the land of my ancestors. I didn't even know what a Basque was. My parents couldn't tell me. When they were being schooled in France, the French government wasn't about to ignite separatism by instructing youth about the mysteries surrounding the origin and culture of the Basques.

At first thought, this may seem to be a big handicap for the writer. Actually, it turned out to be a blessing. The book eventually emerged not as a purely Basque book but as an immigrant book, which explains to me why later I received so many letters from sons and daughters of immigrants of a dozen nationalities—Scandinavian, Scottish and Irish and English, French, Italian, Spanish—all saying that my father's experience was just like their father's experience.

At that time, I had been writing stories for such magazines as the *Saturday Evening Post* and others. It occurred to me that there might be a seed for a story (God knows what kind of story) in my father's return home. I wrote to Peggy Dowst Redmon at the *Saturday Evening Post.*

She very unselfishly thought the story might make for a book instead of a magazine story and introduced me to a literary agency in New York called Curtis Brown, Ltd., a respected agency. Naomi Burton at Curtis Brown sort of signed me up and sent the idea to Harper and Brothers. At Harper's, Elizabeth Lawrence, who was to become almost a legend in her time, wanted to see how I would treat a book.

And so I began to think "book" with trepidation.

So I went. It was an intensely emotional trip. In particular, my father's last good-byes there, because they really were the last good-byes. I in my turn was deeply affected by that country of green mountains, deep oak forests, white stone villages, by my ancestral people. Needless to say, I took notes, tons of them.

But as it turned out, I didn't use a word of them in the writing of the book.

So I had these elements:

A good protagonist, a gentle man who could be dangerous, else he never would have survived in the American West of that time.

Since he was the first of them to go back home, emotional good-byes and messages from the Basque sheepherders he knew here.

Huge amounts of background material on my father's life and experiences in the early West. Too much, by far.

An emotional reunion in the high mountains of the Basque Country with his aged sisters and their families, for whom he had become a legend.

The storytelling about America that goes with all returns to the homeland.

A big question: my role. Should I be a participant or an observer and interpreter?

I really didn't know which way to go. I had been advised by a writer to write a long epic novel. I must have tried a hundred times to start that novel. But every time, I knew there was something missing, and so I would start again.

What was missing, of course, was the poignancy of my father's return to his native land. That, and the discovery I made against my will, finally, that this wasn't a work of fiction. It was actuality. It was nonfiction. It really happened. It wasn't invented.

I was about to give up. I told myself, one more time. If it doesn't work, I will give up. I sat myself down in front of my old Royal portable, inserted that awful blank piece of paper, and sat back in my chair.

After a few moments, my hands unconsciously, without thought or guidance on my part, traveled up to the keyboard and punched out, in lowercase, mind you, this line: "My father was a sheepherder and his home was the hills." I sat back and looked at that line for five minutes before its import came home to me. Then I said to myself, "That's it. You've got a book."

And I did. It started from there. The story felt itself along word by word, line by line, paragraph by paragraph, chapter by chapter. There was no outline. To lock the flow of the story into a framework would have been a disaster. The story found itself.

There were only two moments of pause. I should say that one of those moments lasted for weeks. What happened was this. After I had written four chapters, I sent them into Curtis Brown, my agency, who sent them along to Harper's. Harper's offered me a contract. I went into a state of shock. I kept going back through those chapters, saying to myself, "Laxalt, you must have been doing something right. What was it?"

The second moment of pause was by Harper's.

They were genuinely worried, as I was to learn later. What would happen to the story at the moment of my father's homecoming?

This was the paragraph that relieved their fears and launched the book toward its end:

He was the adventurer who had braved the unknown land across the sea and found his fortune. He was the rebel who had broken the bonds of their own longings and fought the battle and come home victorious. He was the youth who had gone out into the world in beggar's garb and come back in shining armor.

This was the moment of fulfillment. This was the moment of reward he could never have known in America. These were the people who had seen him only when he had set out on his quest, whose vision had not been dulled by nearness through the long trial, and who now saw only the shining armor.

In my turn, there was still one more moment of apprehension. It was where to end the book. Logically, the story should have ended with my father's return to America. That would have completed the circle. It would also have made eminently clear the discovery he had made.

But as I was writing, the story seemed to find its own ending—which was not in America but in the Basque Country. It was so natural that I could not add another chapter, nor another word.

On our next-to-last day there, we had climbed the steep mountain to an ancient house resting in a saddle between forests. We were to have a farewell dinner there, at the home of my father's oldest sister, with an old, lined face, who was cooking the meal in a great black kettle in an open fireplace.

When, finally, we had made our way out of the house and were descending the steep trail, with the song of goodby following down after us, someone began to call, "Come back! Come back!"

I looked at my father, but he did not seem even to have heard. His face was white and grim and violently disturbed, and he was breathing in quick gasps. I reached out and touched him on the arm and said uncertainly, "They want us to come back."

Without turning, he shook his head and cried shakenly, "I can't go back. It ain't my country any more. I've lived too much in America ever to go back." And then, angrily, "Don't you know that?"

And suddenly before me, I saw the West rising up at dawn with an awesome vastness of deserts and mighty mountain ranges. I saw a band of sheep wending their way down a lonely mountain ravine of sagebrush and pine, and I smelled their dust and heard their muted bleating and the lovely tinkle of their bells. I saw a man in crude garb with a walking stick following after with his dog, and once he paused to mark the way of the land. Then I saw a cragged face that that land had filled with hope and torn with pain, had changed from young to old, and in the end had claimed. And then, I did know it.

We walked in silence down the wooded trail, and in a little while the voices died away.

A Man in the Wheatfield

I'M NOT SURE what kind of book I intended to write when I began *A Man in the Wheatfield.* Certainly not what came out of the writing. Words like *allegory,* as it was called by *Time* magazine and the *New York Times,* never crossed my mind, and I would even have laughed if anyone had praised it in such lofty terms when I was writing.

Yet I was always aware, I believe, that the book was more than an ordinary novel. The dreams of evil that made up the theme had been playing around in my mind for quite a while.

I began writing the book in a Basque village in France, though it had nothing to do with Basques or their homeland. I had been writing a novel about Basques in America for more than a year. When we were packing for a move from the seacoast to the high Pyrenees, I had put the sizable manuscript in a footlocker along with other belongings.

The footlocker was already shoved into the Volkswagen bus that was our transportation. The night before our departure, we drove to the city square in Saint-Jean-de-Luz, the fishing port where we had been living for several months. A celebration was under way, and we wanted to see the dancing. We could not have chosen a worse night to park our car with the trunk so visible in the back of the Volkswagen. Being new to the country, we did not know of the raids on such targets by the French *blousons noirs* out of Bordeaux. Our defenses were down, too, because there is no thievery in the Basque Country, where it is considered a crime worse than murder.

When the Basque dancing was over, we went back to the old Volkswagen. To our dismay, we found that a door had been forced open and the footlocker was gone. If I had left the footlocker open, my manuscript would have been ignored and things like cameras and souvenirs taken. Articles of value would have been taken, and the manuscript discarded on the spot. But since the trunk was locked, the thieves had simply taken the entire footlocker.

To track down the French thieves and reclaim the footlocker would have been futile. My manuscript and a year and a half of my writing life had disappeared. I could not reword what had been written. I was left in a state of despair.

Life takes strange turns, and this was one of them. Giving up on the Basque novel, I began writing *A Man in the Wheatfield.* As it turned out, the theft had spurred the writing of a much more important book.

For my setting, I created a small town of Italian immigrants in the desert. The selection of Italians was important. American characters would have been too cynical. I could have used Basques, but their responses to the situations I planned to use were too restrained. Italians, whom I knew well, had the classic qualities I needed for what I was attempting to say.

One was the dream of a child in which he is haunted by an unknown and unseen presence of evil. The second dream is that of the child when he has grown into a young man, a seminarian. In this dream, the unknown presence in the child's nightmare has taken on a shape.

Time magazine described the novel as "a fascinating, ambiguous allegory of men's various ways of confronting fear. Author Laxalt has chiseled out a narrative that is lapidary, unadorned and original."

In the book, Father Savio Lazzaroni knows for a positive fact that there is a devil, and the priest is obsessed with a vision of evil. Mayor Manuel Cafferata, a benevolent and aging despot, is concerned only with his own standing and reputation in the community. Into their small, isolated town of Italian immigrants in the Nevada desert comes a stranger—Smale Calder, the first outsider to set up business in that tightly knit society.

Out of these ingredients noted Stan Paher in a review comes "a stark and chilling tale of human nature and the ways in which people deal with fear and prejudice." When the stranger's secret, single-minded passion for rattlesnakes is revealed, the lives of all involved are changed.

A Man in the Wheatfield was first published by Harper & Row in 1964 to critical acclaim. The book was named one of six notable works of American fiction of that year by the American Library Association, sharing the honor with Ernest Hemingway and Saul Bellow. It was reprinted in England for distribution in the United Kingdom and was translated into Spanish for Spain and South America.

I realize now that while I was writing this book, I was exploring for myself the meanings of such over-used words as *good, envy, ego, hypocrisy, innocence, symbol, myth.*

We all know the meanings of these words. We learned the meanings early—at home, school, church. They were taught to us by our culture. And like all the meanings of words describing the human condition, we don't know them at all, until we have to discover them all over again for ourselves.

This book was my exploration. This was, as Hemingway put it, "all the things you don't know." When it was finished, my own devils dematerialized, evaporated under the harsh light of written exposition. I've never had either dream since.

Time magazine's review that the novel had to do with man's various ways of confronting fears prompted me to see if I had subconsciously been exploring the word *fear.* The subconscious is to me as powerful a force as the conscious, because it does not, or should not, contain learned responses.

My characters:

FATHER SAVIO LAZZARONI, my protagonist and simultaneous antagonist. His consuming fear is the devil.

THE MAYOR, MANUEL CAFFERATA. His fear is of losing people's love and respect, and by that, the loss of position and power.

TONY. He fears the world "out there." Before his service in the army, he knew only this town. He needs a lesson desperately, to understand people, so that he would not fear them anymore. He finds it.

TOSCA. Her fear is of leaving the little town, too. Now that Tony has come back, she won't leave. She is a rebel and a temptress, but she is not dumb.

JOE MORELLI. His fear is that of losing Manuel
Cafferata's favor. He needs Cafferata to lean on.
Still, he cuts Cafferata secretly and mocks him
inwardly. Morelli has lost his standing once when
trying to organize labor at the railroad yards. He
doesn't want to lose it again. He has no courage.
He is much like Cassius, who will stick a knife
into Julius Caesar.

SMALE CALDER. He has no fears, really. He is too
innocent to have any. But he is wary about the
brute snake, who is a full-blown character. The
snake's fear is that Smale Calder will desert him.
He is Smale Calder's conscience. Calder must do
right by him and his own conscience, or suffer
for it. The brute snake knows all about fear. He is
like God.

DELLA SANTA, the banker. His fear is that of losing
his silent struggle for power with Manuel
Cafferata. Della Santa's weapons are money and
appearance, while Cafferata's weapon is his ego.

LUIGI, the retarded boy. Now that he has finally
found a man to identify with, Smale Calder, his
fear is of losing him or incurring his disfavor.

AMADO, the acolyte. A mama's boy who is afraid of the world and blames it for his weakness.

Place is one of the three unities necessary for a dramatic incident. That is the reason for choosing a tiny, isolated community, giving it universality.

All right, our setting is a tiny town made up of Italian immigrants and their children. How would it feel about outsiders? The principal reaction would be resentment, as illustrated by the paranoiac reaction of the butcher, Giometti, at the coming of the "American," Smale Calder.

The people are practical types, farmers and tradesmen. Would they really know or care about abstracts such as evil, as preached by the priest, Father Savio Lazzaroni?

No, they wouldn't care or understand. Father Savio's sermon and the townspeople's reaction demonstrate that.

How does this non-Italian stranger come across so that he is an innocent, natural man who minds his own business?

What is the townspeople's reaction? Suspicion. This is a little town where everybody knows everybody's business.

What part does Smale Calder play in this drama? He is a catalyst. He brings out hidden emotions in the people. Innocence unfortunately does this. Humanity does this. Humanity does not like innocence. People mistrust it.

When I began creating the mayor, Manuel Cafferata, I knew he was important to the story. He could not be just a stick figure.

He became a father symbol to the town. After all, he conceived and created the town. He is strong willed, a doer. But his brush with suicide killed his vision and whatever spirituality he had in him. He can't really see into the future. He trusts people too much. He should have learned the political adage: "I don't know why he hates me; I've never done anything for him."

But, most important, as with all politicians, time has passed him by. Manuel Cafferata has stayed too long.

When writing this book, I built to the first meeting between the mayor and the stranger. I asked myself: how would Manuel Cafferata react to Smale Calder?

At first, the mayor would feel no threat at all to

his standing. He is only surprised and puzzled by Smale Calder. He never understands how Calder causes his empire to fall around him.

Then I asked myself: how about Father Savio? The priest is concerned about his own soul, not that of mankind. He has a real knowledge about the devil, and who is to say that it isn't valid. Remember Hamlet's remark to Horatio on the palace ramparts, after Hamlet has seen his father's ghost, "There are more things in this world than your philosophy and mine have dreamed of, Horatio."

When I created Father Savio, I could not make him all bad. He had to have more than one dimension, that of a priest who saw evil everywhere. I named him Savio to mean a savior of souls. Then I recalled Lazarus, who was rescued from the grave, hence the name Lazzaroni. So Father Savio has the capacity, hidden within himself, to recognize truth. He was both bad and, in the end, good. Smale Calder seems to Father Savio the embodiment of his devil.

Why Amado? I puzzled over that. But I had to create something more than an acolyte, an altar boy. So I made him Tony's opposite, a mama's boy. He is narcissistic, incapable of loving another human. He will learn to hate. And he is a hypocrite, blaming Smale Calder for his own fall from grace by raping Tosca.

What about Tony? He has good instincts. He is able to learn much from Smale Calder, and humankind, through this drama. Before it is over, he sees people for what they are and is afraid of none of them. Tony liked, or rather protected, Amado early. Before this drama is done, he sees the hypocrisy in him. When this scenario is played out, Tony will go out into the world. Because of his idealism, he may meet the same fate as Calder, but he will be a much wiser man than Calder about people and situations. He will know who his enemies are and what their real natures are.

What about the role of the snakes? Are they evil? Of course not. They are used here as a Christian symbol. In Grecian times, the house snake was holy.

In this story, snakes are the innocents of life. Who else is innocent? Calder, of course.

What happens when righteousness confronts innocence? The same fate that Christ underwent in the Crucifixion. Mankind will kill innocence. I wish that I could believe otherwise.

For curiosity's sake, let's project the story and its characters, to see what may happen to them:

Father Savio has been saved from himself. He has seen what he was but recognizes what he is now. Manuel Cafferata will live, and in time be respected again. Morelli, the eternal compromiser, will become a confidant of Della Santa. Tony will leave town. Hopefully, Tosca will join him. Amado will become a bad priest and will finally undo himself. Father Savio will become the best kind of priest, a compassionate man. This episode will happen again, as it always has. Nothing changes.

In a Hundred Graves: A Basque Portrait

WHEN FIRST WE went to live in the Basque Country, I went with the intention of writing about the Basques, but I had no idea what I was going to write. I had no models to follow, yet the ingredients were there for what I wanted to do. The Basques and their country were rich with fresh new material.

I have always been a taker of notes. Memory alone is inadequate. It becomes fuzzy with time. Notes are a blessing in recapturing dialogue and setting and subject matter.

We lived first in Saint-Jean-de-Luz, a fishing

village on the French coast, but spent much of our time driving into the Basque mountains, visiting family and seeing a pure form of Basque life in the villages. It was there that I began taking notes about the people and their way of life. I realized then that whatever I wrote would be drawn from the mountain and village folk. So, when the fall term was done for the children, we moved to the mountain village of Saint-Jean-Pied-de-Port. It was ideal for my writing needs, complete with ramparts, a handball court, a jai alai or *chistera* fronton, and schools for the children. In sum, it was a storybook village.

People and experiences poured over me in a flood. I took voluminous notes on them in the first person. I think I decided then that any intention of writing a novel based on what I was learning was premature. I could never learn enough to write an authentic novel in the few months we would be in the Basque Country. It was then that the idea of a mosaic on Basque village life began to take form. The question of a point-of-view character was solved, and with it the concept of an American Basque seeing his ancestral land became valid. That in turn provided the key to the order of the stories.

I could begin at the beginning and follow the American son through his experiences.

To establish the narrator, I chose a vignette that established: setting, a Basque village; an unfamiliar ritual of tolling the bells for a single death that was an important happening in an uncrowded village. I had introduced the point of view for the stories that followed with "Death in a Basque Village."

The narrator has to have a place to live, so I gave him one in "Our Grand House: Three Views," which introduced the fact of family and a place to move from.

Our children were then introduced, but not in a static statement. I portrayed them in "School in a Fortress," which gave me an opportunity of bringing out setting—a fortified village with ramparts. Also, the children's qualified view of school in a fortress with cold rooms.

With "The House of No Name," I gave to the reader a typical Basque farmhouse and its activities. The story also revealed the narrator's freedom from "the worried world" he had left behind.

"Dominika" provided a companion for the children, also buttressed by a lesson in Basque pride.

"The Perpetual Spring" introduced the women of the village and their interchange of gossip about families, again intermingled with movement in the washing of clothes.

"Our Town Crier" places the reader in time through an ancient medium of recounting the village happenings. I doubt if this medieval practice exists elsewhere.

"The Eyes of the Dove" depicts in narrative form another ancient ritual of the hunt, and more important, the interplay of men from village and farm. Varying facets of Basque character are shown through this story, including humor and cruelty. When the flight of two hundred doves is lured into the nets, the act is not one of cruelty but of ritual. For me, it is a breathtaking event that could invoke condemnation, but, instead, my reaction is one of acceptance.

In "In a Basque Kitchen," the reader is shown the interior of a Basque house, a rare occurrence for anyone not of family. The kitchen is the heart of the house. Table and chairs are oaken and scarred by the use of generations. In its own turn, the fireplace is the heart of the kitchen. Its mantle is adorned copper and pewter pitchers and bowls and an embroidered covering.

It is time now for the narrator to introduce involvement with Basque village life. I was invited to an annual pig killing that would provide most of the household's pork and sausages to last through the winter. I chose to describe the pig slaughter in graphic detail, from the first penning of the pig to the slaughter block. I did this with deliberation, to reveal to the reader the realities of farm life in the Basque Country, down to the bloodletting.

Interspersed with the slaughter was the personal relationship the narrator strikes up with the Basques who had invited him. The native Basques were distantly cool at the outset, but participation in the slaughter broke down the distance and established a kinship. A relationship has been established between the American Basque and the men of the country.

Now that the necessary bases of setting, family, and neighbors had been touched, I was free to write about the unique characters and activities that went to make up the village. I began with "The Basque Troubadour."

The medieval institution of the bard or troubadour is all but lost in Europe. Only in the Basque Country has it managed to survive. The troubadours, or *bertsolariak,* as they are called in Basque, challenge each other in song. They take opposing roles and exchange melody and rhyme. For example, one of the troubadours in my story chose to comment on the life of the shepherd, and the other chose as his subject the life of the *paysan* or peasant. The first singer praises the good life of the shepherd and describes his jealousy of the life of the peasant in his warm house, only to have the illusion destroyed as he peeks into the peasant's house and sees not bliss, but untidiness, brawling children, and a wife beating her husband with a broom for staying out too late to drink with his friends. When the *paysan* or peasant's turn comes, he sings of the good life of the shepherd, which turns into disaster.

And so it went, each troubadour choosing opposing lifestyles and fulfillment and tribulation. They were matching barb for barb.

Neither was declared a winner over his opponent. It was left to the villagers to argue over the quality of the improvising. As for the narrator,

I had gotten a rare glimpse into one of the oldest institutions of the Basques.

The reader having been introduced into the intricacies of village life, I was free to write about whatever intrigued me in the makeup of the village—its participants and its institutions. I chose a healer, a classic handball match, the spectacle of the sheep moving from valley to the high mountains, seasons, and family. The vignettes I chose to write about mingled the satirical ("Homecoming"); the dislike of strangers ("A Peaceful People"); the entertaining ("Theatre of Restraint"); the tradition of market day ("A Newborn Lamb"); the traditional passage of sheep from valley to high mountain ("Bells"); superstition ("The Little People" and "The Hairy God of the Forest"); smuggling ("Victor's Horses"); and a somewhat lengthier tragic romance ("No Crossroads for Agustin"); the German occupation of World War II ("La Guerre Est Terminée"); farm life; and a closing vignette ("Ancestors"), which reflects the narrator's inner feelings about his ancestral land.

And completes the mosaic of Basques in their own milieu.

A Cup of Tea in Pamplona

TO PLACE YOU: the tiny homeland of the Basques—
barely a hundred miles in diameter—straddles the
crest of the western Pyrenees Mountains between
France and Spain. It is a land of deep oak forests,
green mountain valleys, and the rugged seacoasts of
the Bay of Biscay.

In these mountains and on these shores dwell an
ancient people called Basques. Where they come
from, nobody knows. They probably wandered into
the Pyrenees millennia ago, but some scholars claim
they are the pure descendants of Cro-Magnon man,

who evolved in an isolated setting here, fiercely resisting all invaders.

One thing is certain. The Basques are a distinct people who by blood and language are unrelated to the Indo-Europeans who dominated the rest of Europe. The mystery of their origins has never been unlocked.

This novella was not drawn from research in libraries public or private. Oddly enough, there has been very little written about the old, old practice of smuggling over the frontier between France and Spain (except Pierre Loti's *Ramuntcho,* which was a romance novel). I don't know the reason, but I understand.

The same scarcity of written material on the subject holds true throughout most of Europe, notably Switzerland with its many frontiers. I suspect, however, that these countries either don't consider smuggling important, or, if they do, are not too proud of it. They don't want to tell the world about such goings-on.

Whatever the reason, it seemed to me that frontier smuggling would draw interested writers to it like bees to honey. The world of the unlawful and illegal has always attracted the curious. For one example out of many, take the book and screen success of Mario Puzo's *The Godfather*.

In this effort, I was aiming at something more than describing the practice of smuggling in the Basque Country. I was trying to make a social comment on what happens in countries where rich and poor are so sharply divided, or at least where a middle class was not as dominant as in the United States. And where opportunity was then almost nonexistent.

Actually, it's the reason the forebears of most of us left their native countries to come to the United States, the land of opportunity. I'm not getting into what's happening now, but for a long, long time, the Statue of Liberty meant much to the millions who were not born with a silver spoon in their mouths.

I tried to touch on that in this novella, about going to America to get rich. People in the Basque provinces actually believed the legend of American streets paved with gold or the mountains filled with gold nuggets. I tried to argue with them that Americans worked hard for what they managed to gather in their lifetimes. One out of ten believed me.

Back to the story: this novella was written on three levels of comprehension. That's not an exaggeration or an attempt to sound precious. Everything we write has more than one meaning or one level. Take a look at your own stories. Hemingway—of course—had several levels going in *The Old Man and the Sea.*

In *A Cup of Tea in Pamplona,* the surface level is the story of Basque smugglers who lived along the frontier between France and Spain through the centuries until a year or so ago, when the European trade situation evaporated the frontiers and border patrols.

Four of the seven Basque provinces are on the Spanish side of the frontier, three are in France. But don't make the mistake of saying French Basque or Spanish Basque. They are Basque first, last, and always. The political frontier is only a few hundred years old. The Basque Country is millennia old. It is called *Euskal Herria* or *Eskual Herria*—the Land of the Basques.

On the surface level, the story attempts to show how frontier smuggling worked in the Basque

Country, the long tradition it had, the mechanics of smuggling, and the old accords of unwritten agreements between smugglers and frontier guards structured through centuries of confrontation.

On the surface level, I attempted to describe the country and the people in physical terms, necessary because the Basque Country and Basque people are so little known in the world. And of course, to provide the reader with a setting for my story.

As you have seen, the setting is described in glimpses, never in one large package. These glimpses accompany the action line of the story, which is simply the way I like to establish setting so that it is absorbed almost unconsciously by the reader, and, I hope, better remembered that way.

How this writer got his information: My little family and I lived in Basque villages for two years—one year, then a span, then another year. The ingredients for this story came in driblets over those two years. It isn't easy to find out much from the restrained Basques, and it is really tough to find out something that they would prefer not to talk about, such as the practice of smuggling.

As background to the surface story, I had to do a

lot of digging. Smuggling may have been widespread in the Basque Country, but very few people really knew what was going on in the inner circles of smuggling. And smugglers by their nature are close-mouthed.

By using journalistic or curiosity devices, I managed to compile quite a bit of information about the "profession," as I chose to call it in the story. My best source was the fortunate presence of my sort-of uncle-in-law, who had been a police commissar in the past. If we weren't related, he would have told me nothing. But since we were, he provided me with many of the intricacies and mechanics to tell the interior story of smuggling that had never been told in print before.

He even told me of the incident that grew from seed to actuality for this story. That was the code of a death for a death between smuggler and guard. A few years before, a smuggler had violated the code by killing a frontier guard. On the next trip out, the smugglers threw their own man to the wolves. The killing smuggler was caught and shot by the frontier guards.

Other information came from personal observation: frontier guards and big black German guard dogs, descendants from World War II, riding in jeeps on their way to head off a smuggler's passage across the frontier. Actually getting to know some smugglers. They told me nothing, but they revealed their cold and taciturn natures to me. That counted for a lot when I was building characters in my story's smugglers.

I wanted to ask one of the smugglers if I could make a passage across the frontier with him and his men one night. My uncle-in-law said no— emphatically. I would get caught and deported, and the shame would be on his shoulders. Also my family's wrath. Family in America, that is.

There are no secrets kept long among the Basques. Now, conceivably, I could have used this material in an article about smuggling. I chose not to, partly because in a factual news or magazine article, I could use no names or come too close to the facts. With fiction, I had the liberty of using what I wanted. And even smugglers could say that it was fiction and not fact.

Ironically, however, one of the readers of *A Cup of Tea in Pamplona* had word passed to me that I was on track with the inner story of a smuggling passage. That doesn't count for much, but it was amusing to me.

So my information came from oral sources instead of written material. And I actually walked the trails the smugglers used in their contraband passages through the Forest of Iraty and across the mountain frontier, above the timberline between France and Spain. The trails I found by talking to *paysans* along the way and to shepherds on the high mountains. No smuggler could escape their eyes. They had the long vision of eagles.

Basque smugglers weren't passing cocaine and heroin. That was forbidden, and the Basques themselves would have turned in anyone who did.

The second level of the story was to come up with a plot line for what was in some ways an adventure story, to construct a vehicle through which I could bring my material to light.

Essentially, the plot line at this level is: A man named Gregorio is an old Basque smuggler. He crosses the frontier from France to Spain. Through an accident of recognition, he inadvertently manages to alert the frontier guards to a very possible smuggling passage. This creates the first aura of suspense for the action line.

In a small café in neighboring Spain, Gregorio tells his Spanish Basque counterpart, a man named Fermin, that he is tired and thinking of retiring. This is important. This is the planted seed of what this novella is all about.

Gregorio needs a replacement. He is thinking of his own helper, a man named Nikolas. Fermin asks the key unexpected question. He asks how poor Nikolas is. The planted seed begins to form shoots.

The plans for the passage are made, but they are of secondary importance here.

Gregorio returns to his Basque province in France and meets with Nikolas. He makes Nikolas the offer to take over as chief. Any other smuggler would have jumped at it. Nikolas doesn't. To Gregorio's surprise, and anger, Nikolas wants to think it over. The seed now has grown into a full-blown conflict.

Gregorio lectures Nikolas with an eloquent little bit of wisdom in which is contained the heart of this story: "What we call respectability is a foolish little game the poor must play in order to hold themselves equal to the rich, who are seldom respectable."

Briefly, the rest of the plot line: Nikolas recruits his helpers. Three reliable ones and one firecracker, Luis, his brother-in-law. Luis's coming on the trip adds another menace.

A Jeep caravan of frontier guards goes through the village. They are alerted, posing still another menace.

The smugglers make their passage. Nikolas and the two good men show up at the rendezvous. Luis manifests his menace by not showing up. When he does appear, we learn that he has killed a guard dog, bearing out what we feared.

The smugglers run into the frontier guards. Luis uses his knife to commit the unpardonable crime—that of killing a frontier guard.

This is the climax of the story. Nikolas makes the big decision. He hands Luis the guard's pistol. Luis knows what that means. He has been sentenced to death.

The remainder of the story is the denouement. The story threads are unraveled. Nikolas meets with

Gregorio. Nikolas and his wife break with her family. There is the charade of an auction in the village square. Nikolas comes out of the closet—he has succeeded Gregorio as a patron of smuggling.

On the third level, the real story of *A Cup of Tea in Pamplona*: I have written about a social structure and humans that I was confronted with, a Basque story. But the mores and traditions are or were universal in all European societies before the middle class and its values began to spread throughout the world.

Actually, the Basques' social structure of a sharp division between rich and poor was less defined in this little pocket of Europe. This was the birthplace of democracy. When the Romans in their conquest of the world came to the Basque Country, they found something that had only been dreamed about by the Greek philosophers, a working democracy in which the people elected their rulers. A feudal system did not exist among the Basques. Feudal lords did not attain their position by right of inheritance or blood succession, like the House of Hapsburg, for example. And the much touted rights of man that triggered the French Revolution and the American Revolution had existed for ages in the

Basque Country. They were called *fueros* in the Basque provinces of Spain and *fiers* in the Basque provinces of France.

Among the Basque people, serfdom did not exist. A man had to be paid for his work. He was not a slave. And no man was really superior to another. All Basques regarded each other as equal in station. I have tried to demonstrate that by Nikolas's fury with his landlord about the price paid for a meal, and even by Nikolas in his confrontation with the chief smuggler, Gregorio.

So what does the social division come down to here? What standards?

Money. Level of wealth. Opportunity. Bettering one's station. If a man's father is a cobbler, then the traditional society decreed that he must be a cobbler, too. In the time this story was written, I was dealing with a social structure that equated "a good name" with no name at all, a mountain agrarian society that withered hope by its collective inscrutable scrutiny.

To avoid that scrutiny, one must keep station and appearance. For a peasant to break the code of station is disaster in intangible ways.

I love the Basque Country and its people, but that does not preclude me from making my own conclusions about what I don't like.

Things have changed greatly since this book was written. The young Basques of today are mobile. They can migrate to Paris or Madrid and find opportunity.

On this level, the internal level, let's examine the human element:

What is the character of the smuggler chief, Gregorio? He is a proven leader of men and a good judge of character. He is tired, and he wants to retire. He is gray all over. He is a completely dispassionate man with a wry sense of humor about the society he lives in. He knows the strengths and weaknesses of smugglers. He voices this wisdom in the paragraph where he says, "How alike the smugglers are, good chests, a little hunger, an elastic conscience most importantly."

As we are introduced to Gregorio, we sense very little turmoil in his conscience. His son has entered a seminary to become a priest and thereby absolve his father's sins.

Gregorio is a practical man. Lacking his son, he

needs someone to take over his business. That man may be Nikolas.

Nikolas is steady, dependable, and quiet. He is a tenant farmer with a wife and two children. He has been a smuggler's helper to make extra money. He has done this secretly, so he is still a member of society in good standing. The offer from Gregorio gives him pause despite the promise of riches. If he accepts the offer, he must decide to come out of the closet, to go public. Nikolas hesitates because of the risk of losing his good name. Preserving a "good name" in this society means following the code, not rising above one's station monetarily. He must also avoid the gossip and the stigma that go with becoming publicly known as a smuggler.

In this book, I left it to the reader to judge for himself whether Nikolas is a moral man when we first meet him, and why or why not. We must remember that, having made smuggling trips for Gregorio, Nicolas is, as the saying goes, a little bit pregnant. Still, he has made these trips against his better judgment for the welfare of his family.

The wife of Nikolas plays a small but important role in this drama. She is slovenly and pleads poverty, but that should not prevent her from seeing that her children have washed their faces. She cares only for public appearance and respectability. She portrays envy for unearned wealth. She has a table-cloth but doesn't even bother to use it for Gregorio. She yearns for the riches that America offers through marriage to one of her children when they emigrate, so that they can support her in the manner she wants. We are left to suspect that despite her "good name," she has been an influence in Nikolas's decision to become a smuggler's helper. Despite her good name, she asks no questions about where the extra money comes from.

Nikolas is left to think over his options. He rationalizes being a smuggler's man by the fact that he has so little money and that the only victim is the government, for which the Basques care little.

How did the story come to be?

I was helping my cousin and his hired hand plant corn on one of the farms my cousin owned. I knew there was to be an auction of contraband horses in the village square, so I was impatient. I wanted a certain little mare. The hired hand seemed to know quite a bit about smuggling, and I sensed that he was a smuggler's helper.

Now, I had been wondering where to start and who the central figure should be in a smuggling story. I found him. I watched the hired hand. He was quiet and Herculean in strength. The farmhouse he lived in was terrible. He had a wife and two kids. He was poor. So I found my central character, Nikolas. I wondered what he would do if he became a chief of smugglers.

The story grew from there. Gregorio actually lived and was the main smuggler in the village. I had found my old smuggler who wanted to retire. He looked and acted in real life just like Gregorio in the story. A leader. Dispassionate. Tired.

So I had my two central characters.

Nikolas's wife and kids and the farmhouse fell into place. Even the conversation about America. As she talked, I saw that respectability meant the world to her. Her and her husband's good name were all they had.

But Gregorio can't be one-dimensional, so I added the fact that his son had gone to seminary to absolve his father's sins. Gregorio tries to make light of it, but this doesn't work. He is hurt. Here is the flaw in his character.

The other characters were easy: Luis, the troublemaker. I actually saw the incident where he struck another *paysan,* breaking his nose. I had found my catalyst. I gave him another tie—brother of Nikolas's wife. A trap for Nikolas, and finally his undoing.

The smuggler's other helpers were minor. They actually existed and were smuggler's helpers, too.

The locales: I had traveled the roads to Spain and seen and talked to frontier guards going through. So I knew them. I had eaten in the nonadvertised restaurant on a trip to Roncevalles or Ronceveau. While I ate, I saw fierce young Basques in a whispered conversation. One man dominated them. A man with a moustache. Immensely strong and immensely dependable. I had found my Fermin, Gregorio's counterpart in Spain.

The horses: They had come through the village with the frontier guards who caught them. I went to the corral to look them over.

I had been through the forest route that Nikolas took. I had been to the ancient shepherds' hut high above the timberline of the Pyrenees several times. I had climbed over that green and brutal rim that divides France and Spain, so I didn't have to imagine that.

The restaurant where Nikolas and his men eat in the village I had been to many times, so I knew that. I knew Gregorio's house because we rented it while we were there. I knew the cemetery. It is the first place to go if you want to learn about the people.

I put the offer of being chief of smugglers to Nikolas in my own mind and wondered what he would do. He valued his good name. I asked myself: what does a good name mean in this society? To follow the code. Not to rise above one's station monetarily. The avoidance of gossip.

These would be the obstacles to his accepting Gregorio's offer and getting rich.

Nikolas's wife: I went back with my cousin and talked to her. She was so righteous, but righteousness was all she had. She didn't like being poor. I asked myself: Well, she knows that Nikolas is "a little pregnant" as a smuggler's helper. Does it bother her? No. The money is important, so she is guilty of hypocrisy. But that is necessary, too.

Nikolas is tormented. This is a good man.

When the boy loses the coin that falls through the crack, a crisis is reached. Sick at heart, Nikolas decides that he must act to feed and clothe his family.

Nikolas dreams. He sees the little dangers appearing to him, but when he was a child. Why a child? It is a return to the clear vision of childhood.

What does the dance mean? Actually, it is probably the oldest stylized folk dance in Europe. Ballet has even borrowed a step from it, the *pas de Basque*. The dance originated in my father's high mountain province. I moved it here. I had wanted to use it for years but never found the proper place. I had found it now. The meaning of the dance is lost to antiquity. They say now that if the wine is spilled, it will mean bad fortune for the village. I took the liberty of changing it to bad fortune for the head dancer, who in the story is Nikolas.

What do these unusual dancers mean? One: the musician with the cape and silver flutes? He calls the tune to which men dance in this life.

Two: the standard-bearer? He represents the immutable standards or mores of society.

Three: the man-woman? The duality in all of us. From the woman, caution in human nature; from the man, determination to do his duty.

Four: the cat man? He carries the wooden scissors to clip the threads of fate. In this story, he clips the threads that support man. He leaves man to his own free will. He forecasts disaster and the fate of the head dancer, the Zamalzain, the Centaur, the man-horse.

Five: the head dancer? He is vain above all others. He is reckless and overconfident. He risks too much. He goes too far. (This story was written before I ever read *The Old Man and the Sea*.)

But in this drama, the head dancer pays the ultimate price. When he tips over the goblet of wine, he is put to death by the other dancers.

What does the dance mean? Man cannot go too far on his own without censure. Society in every form has its celebrities until they are visibly flawed, until they make the fatal misstep.

How does this apply to Nikolas? He knows that if he makes a wrong decision now, he will lose society's supporting threads. He knows also that one day, he must pay the price for his decision to go too far.

Does Nikolas gain anything by his taking over as chief of smugglers?

That depends on what the reader thinks. Nicholas makes money, of course. But will it be worth the loss of his good name?

From a secretly immoral man, Nikolas will become a publicly immoral man. We are left to wonder if Nikolas will be able to accept the consequence of that.

In conclusion, we must ask whether this story has a hero. As author, I must say not really. Then why did I write this story?

I set out to reveal what can happen to a good person prevented by society from bettering himself. Though it may seem so, the story is not one of morality, but rather of immorality. The tone is not bitter. It is written with compassion for an individual whose adversary is a world of no hope, of grinding poverty. He takes the choice offered to him, not to be ground under any longer.

Genesis of a Trilogy

The Basque Hotel

WHEN ONE UNDERTAKES a trilogy, he is faced
with two basic questions:

Where should it begin?

Where should it end?

The choices of beginning and end were over-
whelming. I was dealing with lifetimes and a hundred
turning points and climaxes in those lifetimes.
Since I wanted to write about an immigrant Basque
family, the trilogy should logically have begun in the
Basque Country from which my parents emigrated
and followed their lives chronologically to America
and in America. I chose instead to start the trilogy

by introducing the point-of-view character in America. I chose to make him a youth so that there would be a freshness in the people and things encountered. The story is mostly autobiographical, and the narrator is a boy named Pete, whose experiences and emotions are mine.

Most important, the story is already in motion, and hopefully, the reader is caught up in the motion. Immediacy is inherent, and the authenticity of the trilogy is founded.

In the opening volume, we are introduced to Carson City, the setting for most of the trilogy, and we get to know a number of its characters—politicians, merchants, Indians, and cowboys. We are introduced to the State Capitol and its symbolic and actual presence for a good part of the action. We get to know Main Street and its shops and stores and poolroom. The unique characters that inhabit every small town, it seems, add color and humor to the story. Our story has such as Buckshot Dooney and George Washington Lopez, the town drunks.

Brothers and sisters play their family roles, and we are part of a typical immigrant family.

The facets of Pete's character are shaped throughout the first volume—his love of adventure, his first taste of injustice, his fixation on the town drunks, his dislike of cruelty, his fear of authority in the form of prohibition agents, his taunting of authority, his witnessing of racial prejudice against Indians, his father's admission to bootlegging.

When winter comes, Pete ventures into the deep snow mountains in search of a Christmas tree, that American symbol his immigrant parents are ignorant of. He almost loses his life in the search, but survives only to weaken himself by a crippling disease—rheumatic fever. In his confinement, Pete draws closer to his brothers and sisters and gets to know the town characters who come to visit him—Mizoo the cowboy, Hallelujah Bob, Pansy Gifford, and Buckshot Dooney. Through them, we learn the character of Carson City.

Pete recovers from his bout with rheumatic fever, but his heart will always be scarred. Still, he convinces his mother that he be permitted to go to his father's mountain sheepcamp on horseback. Pete is introduced to the life his father has led and learns to love the mountains. But there are bitter lessons to be learned, too. Pete is growing up.

When school starts again, Pete establishes stature when he wins a fight. He also loses his virginity in a summer night's game. But he must pay the penalty and confess his sin in an agonizing session with the priest.

Depression comes, and Pete learns the lesson of shame. His mother is hospitalized, and the children of the family suffer the gentle tyranny of life under his father's brother, Uncle Joanes.

Pete's boyhood comes to an end when the old hotel burns to the ground. He watches it burn and knows that the growing-up part of his life has ended. This is symbolized when he wanders from the burning hotel to the shack where he and his playmates had played at war. Among the rubble is a sword that had once been his in the days of glorious war, when he had imagined it to be a shining sword. He laughs and casts it aside, and with it, his boyhood.

Child of the Holy Ghost

Since the mother figure is the actual founder of the immigrant family, it would have been logical to start the trilogy with her story. This would have accomplished explaining the roots of the family in their original foreign setting, revealing the character of the Basques, and providing the reason the mother, Maitia, chose to leave her native country.

I chose not to use the mother's story as the beginning of the trilogy. I was writing for an American audience and attempting to show the emotional experiences of my generation of the immigrant story. Also, the story is set in motion with the attitudes of a first-generation American, the background from which he sprung, and the reason he acts the way he does.

In *Child of the Holy Ghost,* the young Pete is now a man and the narrator of his mother's story. Being a scholar and writer, he is equipped to undertake the involved mystery of his mother's birth. We learn immediately that she is illegitimate, but we don't know how this came to be. Pete is the intermediary who will unravel the mystery of what happened in the Old Country and provide the reader with the resolution of her life.

His search for the answer is purposely involved, so that the reader accompanies Pete in his search through the curtain of village secrecy. The story actually begins with his mother's mother, Jeanne, a beautiful but willful protagonist. Jeanne falls in love with a French agricultural specialist from Paris, son of a distinguished family. Jeanne becomes pregnant, but she cannot marry the French Arnaud because he is already married. Instead, she is forced into marriage with a wealthy aspiring Basque named Labadiste. When the child is born, her raising becomes the responsibility of her grandparents. Jeanne accompanies Labadiste to Argentina, where he is involved in importing young Basques from France to work on the ranches of Argentina.

Maitia is born and raised in the village and her mother's ancestral home. Her grandfather Garat is prepared to dislike the child he has promised to raise, but he learns to love her intensely.

As for Jeanne, she has been abandoned by her lover. She has to bear their child, and she is expected to leave the child as soon as it is weaned. She must leave the village forever, marry Labadiste, and go to a country she knows nothing about. She must forget that the child of her bearing ever existed.

Jeanne returns from Argentina to her ancestral

home. She is reunited with her illegitimate daughter, Maitia. The old scandal of her affair is resurrected, and Maitia becomes the victim of village gossip and condemnation by the Church. Jeanne knows it is time to take her child away to Bordeaux, where she lives with Labadiste.

In part two, we meet the shepherd boy, Petya, who lived and worked for an old shepherd grazing sheep on the great mountain humps that divide France from Spain.

By accident, the boy, Petya, had seen a file of smugglers emerging from the mist. One of the smugglers has betrayed the rest. The smuggler chieftain murders him by catapulting him off the precipice. Petya is witness to the murder. From then on, his life is in danger. The smuggler chieftain must do away with Petya. The youth tells the old shepherd what he has seen. The old shepherd tells Petya that he must run away before he is killed. The smuggler chieftain cannot afford to let him live as a witness to the murder. Petya reluctantly leaves that same night, descending the grassy slopes and traversing the deep forest, until he comes to his family home. He tells his family of his dilemma, and that he must leave the Basque Country and go to America to save his life.

Maitia's relationship with her grandfather Garat grows intense. She becomes loved by the village and takes care of Garat. A young man of the country becomes attached to Maitia, and Garat is terrified of losing her. He makes a will that is intended to protect her, giving her the farm and the house, so as to bind her to the Garat homestead. In so doing, he passes over his son, Jean Baptiste.

Petya has become a sheepherder in America, braving the storms and solitude of the High Sierra. He dreams often of home, of the old shepherd who trained him, and of their high stone cabin.

Maitia establishes her sovereignty over the Garat homestead. Her uncle, Jean Baptiste, feels he has been cheated and calls her a bastard. His friend the mayor warns him to mind his ways and play a waiting game. The mayor infers that he can be instrumental in overturning the will.

In part four, we see Petya's life in the mountains. He has decided to go home to the Basque Country. Laborde, the owner of the sheep outfit, warns him against it. World War I has broken out, and Petya is sure to be conscripted and sent to the front.

In the Basque Country, Maitia is visited by her half brother, Michel, who is on his way to the German front. He could have stayed behind the lines, but his pride would not let him. Despite Maitia's pleading, Michel goes to the German front.

In America, Petya is taken from the hills to Reno after an absence of five years. He still fully intends to return to France and the Basque Country, but in the hotel, he learns that he will be arrested and conscripted by French authorities if he returns. He rethinks his rejection of a job offer with a promised partnership with Laborde, the Basque sheepman.

In France, Maitia has gone to Bordeaux to stay with her dying mother. While she is gone, her uncle, Jean Baptiste, and the mayor, Chaco, are successful in their efforts to overturn Garat's will. Maitia is told by the judge of his decision. She has clearly been cheated, and the Garat farm and house will go to Jean Baptiste. Maitia has no choice but to leave.

She goes to Bordeaux to live in Labadiste's hotel and stay with her sisters. She receives a letter from her beloved brother, Michel, who, after an argument with his father, has gone to America. But he is not strong enough to become a sheepherder. His health deteriorates, and he is left jobless.

Maitia shows the letter to Labadiste. His resistance crumbles, and he commissions Maitia to go to America and bring his son home. Maitia leaves France. When she reaches San Francisco, she learns that Michel is in a hospital in Reno. She goes to him.

In the hospital, Michel has struck up a relationship with Petya, who is recovering from injuries he suffered when he was bucked off a horse. Maitia meets Petya, and a love affair blossoms. By this time, Petya has decided to stay in America and work for Laborde, the Basque sheepman, and eventually becomes a part owner of Laborde's land and animal holdings. Michel dies, and Maitia marries Petya.

The story ends with a jump into my generation. The oldest son, Leon, becomes a successful lawyer and is elected governor of Nevada. He is invited to France to be honored. He must also visit Donibane, his mother's village. Pete tells Leon their mother's story and elicits a promise from him. He will

denounce the mayor who was instrumental in disin-
heriting Maitia for her illegitimacy.

Leon does so, and the score is settled. Maitia
dies, dreaming of her Basque Country and the farm
on which she was raised. Her final thoughts are the
illusions of returning home.

The Governor's Mansion

The Governor's Mansion is the third and final book of
the Basque Family Trilogy. It completes the classic
circle of the immigrant to the United States.

The setting for this volume is Nevada, where the
family has settled. Maitia's sprawling house in
Carson City, the capital, is the jumping-off place
for the book's action.

World War II has ended, and the four brothers
of Maitia's progeny have settled in western Nevada.
One of the daughters has married and settled in
California, and the eldest daughter, a nun, is situated in a convent in Las Vegas.

The four brothers have established a ritual of going to their mother's home in Carson City for Fri-
day lunches. Through the grown-up years, they have

remained close to each other. Three have become lawyers, and the fourth son, Pete, is attached to the University of Nevada in Reno.

The central figure in this book is the eldest son, Leon, who has become a successful lawyer. Along the way, he has become intrigued by the world of politics. He was elected as district attorney in Carson City, but politics paled for him and he is now a full-time practicing lawyer with his own firm.

Leon summons his brothers to a family luncheon at their mother's home in Carson City. (The family luncheon is exactly as it happened in actuality. There was no need for heightening of drama. It was inherent in the scene. Even the dialogue was as it is related in the book.)

Leon has an announcement to make. He has been asked to run for lieutenant governor of Nevada, by none other than the incumbent lieutenant governor, a former silent-screen movie actor who lives in Las Vegas and has announced that he is going to run for governor. Leon asks for reactions from his three brothers. Each for his own reason is skeptical.

Their father excuses himself from the conversation and goes outside to chop wood. He shows no interest in the political decision to be made. The mother, Maitia, is surprisingly skeptical. This comes as a surprise to the brothers, particularly Pete, who knows her passion for respectability and what produced that passion.

The pros and cons of Leon's running for office are hashed out in candid terms. Whatever the brothers think, it is academic. It is obvious that Leon is going to run for the office of lieutenant governor.

At first glance, the campaign issue would seem to be of less than dramatic proportion. After all, Nevada is the least-populated state in the nation, and the presumption has to be that it is rural in lifestyle and attitude. But one element sets the state and its politics apart from the rest—the presence of glitzy Las Vegas, luxurious hotels, and the presence of the Mafia. The legacy of mobster Bugsy Siegel is very much alive.

Leon listens to the arguments for and against. Although he seems undecided, the brothers know he will run.

Now that the story is set in motion, I decided to depart from the plot and soliloquize. This was by design. I wanted the reader to know what was involved in politics, what politics was about. The political novels I had read, and there are not many (*All the King's Men* being a superior exception), usually had a predictable plot from beginning to end. In my opinion, the reader emerged not knowing anything of depth about politics. I wanted to stress the interior message that this is what politics is about, this is how it works, these are the types of people and situations that one encounters in a political campaign.

What children we were. Because we had grown up knowing politicians, we thought we knew politics. But all we had really known was the outward face of politics. We had seen the affable smile and felt the firm handclasps, but we had never seen the unguarded moment when the smile was gone and the bruising showed through, and we had not even wondered why these men grew old before their time.

We had seen the outward face, but we had never been privy to those secret rooms where that face was manufactured. We had heard the roar from beyond the podium, but we had never listened to the muted voices that dissected and plotted the oratory.

We had taken it for granted that a man in politics either wins or loses, but we had never considered that there is no middle ground in politics. We were in a game where there is a winner and there is a loser. To have almost won meant nothing but to have lost. A political man rises to the battle and survives, or he falls away into oblivion.

We learned that it was not enough simply to declare for office. That was only the beginning and the easiest part of it all. It was not enough to say, "I am a candidate because I believe . . . and to think to yourself, *You must be able to see that I have strong beliefs.*" But the electorate is not clairvoyant and in every American there is a Missourian that must be shown the mule. From there come the interminable meetings in the secret rooms, where the mechanics of the message are painfully hammered out.

We learned there was no escape from the circus that is American politics—the showmanship of billboards and signs and bumper stickers, the revival meetings that are called political rallies, the modulated voice of radio and the theatrics of television, and above all, the sustaining of momentum.

We learned the parry and thrust of infighting, that there was a right time to attack, a right time to defend, and, most important, a right time to keep still.

We learned that it was a time for the diminishing of ego, because every thought, word, and deed must become subservient to the campaign and all egos must be diminished in order to preserve the almighty ego of the candidate.

We learned that the electorate does not give a damn about issues, that a warm smile and a handshake, a good radio voice, and a television presence mean more than all the issues put together. We learned finally that there are no merits in campaigns, but only show biz.

We learned that a campaign means people— people to speak well of you, people to arrange rallies, people to put up signs, and people to pay for all this. And this last was the hardest of all, because for every one who gave you money out of good heart, with no strings attached, there was another who would consider it a due bill he expected to collect in time.

We were hurt when people we thought were friends suddenly took pains to avoid us, and it took a long time to understand that their pocketbooks were involved and that political party or a job in jeopardy could override the friendship of a lifetime. We were puzzled when others who had never spoken to us before now began to speak to us for an ulterior motive, the promise of reward.

And then there were the people who made it worthwhile, the friends who stayed by you at great risk and the ones who appeared out of nowhere, who believed in you and worked for you, who had everything to lose but would ask for nothing in return.

For the first time, we felt the ridicule of opposition newspapers in public print for everyone to read and hear the private things about family that might have been whispered before in a few places but were now spoken aloud in many places, rumors embellished and rumors invented. And we endured the fury and helplessness of all this, because there was nothing we could do about it.

We learned what the testing by fire can do to men who live the intensity of six years in the six months of a campaign, who grow ten feet tall or diminish to nothing.

We learned that uncertainty and the intangible are the ghosts that stalk every campaign, and it is like fighting with shadows or walking in quicksand because you are never sure whether you are winning or losing or even know exactly where you stand.

What children we were. But, like children, we learned quickly.

The soliloquy is sobering, aimed at instructing the reader about what is involved in the game of politics. We learned what the immigrant family must be prepared to face.

As contrast to this serious side of politics, I chose deliberately to draw from its humorous aspects. Purposeful or not, politics abounds with humorous incidents and characters. To initiate the reader to this element of humor, I began the political action with a setting and characters that were humorous—

i.e., the not-quite-bright candidate for governor, a one-time silent-screen movie star named Tex Maynard, and a politically cynical advisor, George Friar. They engage in an altercation that injects humor into a politically serious situation—the opening strategy of the campaign. Again, I did not have to invent the confrontation. This was exactly the way it happened.

The tactics of politics now begin to unfold: the obligatory suntan gleaned from reclining at swimming pools, learning how to drink at rallies without getting drunk, riding a horse in a parade to show the western identification, learning how to remember names—all tactics aimed at the rural or cowboy country vote.

The scene changes abruptly to Las Vegas, its glitzy resort-hotel setting, its eastern-bred Mafia characters.

With this move, I was breaking new ground in Nevada literature—fiction and nonfiction. Even historians had shied away from mentioning the presence of mobsters and mob-financed luxury hotels. I was not walking uncertain ground, however. As a United Press correspondent and now, as an aide and brother to a major political candidate, I had gotten to know the Las Vegas scene, which was fertile in settings and characters like dealers, pit bosses, cocktail waitresses, and hookers. I used them in full measure, employing their alien backgrounds and manners of speech.

To my surprise, a new element began to emerge. It was that of a code of mores for gangsters, which humanized them for the reader.

Our protagonist, Leon, is plunged into the Las Vegas scene and copes with it. His running mate, Tex Maynard, drops dead, and Leon is plunged into a race for the governorship, a race beset with money problems and the obstacles of such political problems as name identification. Leon solves his problems with ingenious new tactics in the game of political campaigning. He takes to television and homey spot announcements about his family. The show is a success, and *Leon's Hour* becomes an institution.

Leon weathers the machinations of Las Vegas politics and is elected governor. The first foray of the immigrant son in American politics is accomplished.

Leon's tenure as governor is to be unlike those of his ranching and mining predecessors. His alliance with syndicate members Moe Dalitz and Ruby Kolod is revealed ominously at the end of part 1.

In part 2, Leon's tenure in office is marked by a secret session with J. Edgar Hoover in his campaign to better relations between Nevada and the FBI. I used the secret session in toto, revealing a quirky Hoover and his view of the Kennedy clan. But Leon's mission is successful. Relations between Nevada and the Federal Bureau of Investigation are healed.

The mysterious advent of eccentric billionaire Howard Hughes dominates Leon's incumbency. Leon weathers the frenzied intrigue that follows and steers Howard Hughes into buying seven Mafia-controlled resort hotels on the Las Vegas Strip. The day of the hoodlum ownership of Las Vegas is ended.

Much had happened in the three years since Tex Maynard dropped dead. Leon had been elected. Howard Hughes's empire headquarters had moved to Nevada. The Mafia had moved out. Kirk Kerkorian, the airline magnate, had offered Leon the presidency of MGM, which would have meant resigning the governorship. Leon, torn with the decision, had opted in favor of duty and declines the offer.

Politics has taken its toll on the immigrant family. The father, bereft of the company of his sons, is lonely. The mother's house, which prized its privacy, has been invaded.

Leon and Pete join their father for a cleansing stay at the mountain sheepcamp. The father's deteriorating health makes itself evident, and the patriarch of the immigrant family soon dies.

Howard Hughes, the reclusive billionaire, continues to be the dominant factor in Leon's incumbency. Since I was privy to the unpublicized machinations of the Hughes organization, I decided to use nearly everything I knew in my story.

As for Leon, he welcomes Hughes's coming to Nevada, because it could mean the exodus of the Mafia as hotel owners and gambling magnates. Leon and Hughes become friends via long-distance telephone, because Hughes refuses to meet anyone in officialdom face-to-face, including the governor. Hughes confides to Leon that he sees no visitors because of his deteriorating physical appearance.

Leon is forced, out of party duty, to run for the U.S. Senate. Leon and Pete hit the campaign trail through Nevada's rural towns. Leon's opponent is Senator Jack Horner, a man of doubtful credentials. Leon's aides uncover Horner's corruption and publicize it.

In a narrow election race, Leon actually wins, but shenanigans in the Las Vegas county clerk's office cheat him of the victory.

The family gathers at their mother's home in Carson City. There are mixed reactions of anger and relief.

Pete knows that Leon will run again for the U.S. Senate, but Pete will not be there to help him. He has seen as much of politics as he wanted to.

A brief postscript of a dream of Pete's reveals his conviction of the transitory quality of fame. The pure immigrant dream has come to an end.

POSTSCRIPT

The Library and I

IN THE YEARS of my growing up in tiny Carson City, the Nevada State Library was my second home. In the 1930s, it was situated in the octagonal little annex to the State Capitol.

It goes without saying that libraries of any kind were scarce in the Nevada of the Depression era. Books were expensive and hard to come by, and public libraries were rare adjuncts to the small towns that peopled our state. Only the affluent or dedicated book lovers were fortunate enough to have private libraries in their homes.

Because it was the capital of Nevada, Carson City was favored. State government could not be considered complete without libraries and archives. So we were the beneficiaries of that requisite.

The Nevada State Library, of course, was dominated by books dealing with the history, people, and economics of the state. It was almost too much to expect that the library would contain a considerable wealth of books for the general public, but ours did. The classics of literature were to be found there for the literary-minded of the citizenry.

But who would expect that a governmental institution would also contain *Tarzan of the Apes*? But contain it the State Library did, plus a hundred other volumes for young readers such as I.

My memory fails me when I try to recall who first told me about the library and Tarzan. But once bitten, whole new worlds opened for me. I could travel on the wings of imagination through the jungles of Edgar Rice Burroughs and his adventures of Tarzan, with James Oliver Curwood and Jack London over the frozen wastes of the Yukon, and with Albert Payson Terhune and the wonderful collies of Sunnybrook Farm. In short, through the adventure books of a century of literature aimed at the young readers of yesterday.

I developed an insatiable appetite for all these treasures. Even in summers when I went to the desert and mountain sheepcamps of my father, Nevada State Library books went with me. Inevitably, when I returned the books to the library, they were well scented with the aroma of sagebrush. This bothered the tastes of the two lady librarians, not young, who dressed in the accepted fashion of their time, lace collars and cuffs and elaborate pompadour hairdos. But in time, they learned to accept it. I suspect that the books I checked out in the summers underwent a thorough airing before they were put back on the shelves.

I came away from my days in the Nevada State Library with memories of musty bookshelves and towering columns of books. These memories will stay with me always.

But equally as important a legacy given to me by the Nevada State Library was the love of writing that would become the consuming passion of my life.

Along with flights of imagination, I had learned the gift of story telling.

In my writing life, nothing has equaled that gift and legacy—the magic of words.

The Writing Life

ONCE HAVING DECIDED back then to become a writer, I hadn't the remotest idea of what was involved in the writing life. As a boy just growing into adulthood, I knew no writers, nor had I ever read anything about the lives they led.

I knew nothing about what a writer writes, how a writer lives, how much money he makes, where a writer goes to find things to write about, what makes a story, what is the difference between writing for magazines and books—both of which were in short supply in our immigrant household—and most important of all, where and to whom a writer goes for enlightenment on these myriad questions.

I was to learn the answers through the years of growing up and the years that followed. They came in a slow and often painful process that never ended. I suspect they will continue to come all of a writer's life, until the day he puts his pen aside for the last time.